Dear Blooming Me,
By Amadora Fernández

The story where I left to forget him
and came back finding me…

Dear Blooming Me

Copyright © 2018 by Amadora Fernández
All rights reserved. This book or any portion thereof may not be reproduced or used in any manner whatsoever without the express written permission of the publisher except for the use of brief quotations in a book review.

First edition, 2018
English E-Book ISBN: 978-1-9999733-2-2
English printing ISBN: 978-1-9999733-0-8

Editing by Dinah Heybourn

Visit www.amadorafernandez.com

ACKNOWLEDGEMENTS

To my father, for his unconditional support. Dad, I owe you who I am and what I have. You have taught me to fight, to be strong, to look forward, to be honest, to have faith, to not give up and to love with all my heart. You have taught me about the concept of family and to take care of mine. You have been my engine and, although I cannot imagine the rest of my life without you, you can be sure that I will wake up every day with a smile, my head up and I will walk forward like you have always taught me.

To my mother, for her strength and perseverance. Mum, you have far exceeded all our expectations: as a mother, as a wife, as a professional and as a strong woman. I never stopped having faith that you would come back to life and seeing you smile makes my world. You are and always will be my companion, the voice of my conscience and the hand that will bring me back up.

Dear Blooming Me

Introduction

Like many people who decide to travel alone, I was lost. My ex-boyfriend had broken up with me and, although I did not realise it at the time, it had opened the big Pandora's Box that I had been filling with fears, worries and problems over the last five years. I was aware that after a break-up you go through a few sad months, until one day you wake up and accept it, and get back to your life. But I wanted to speed up the process. For first time in my life, I allowed myself to be sad. I allowed myself to be so sad that I brought past burdens and feelings to the surface, turning my mind to negative thoughts such as, "Why does this have to happen to me?" or, "Have I not gone through enough in the last five years?" I allowed myself to feel weak and lost.

One Monday in May, walking back home from the office in London, I thought, "If I could be doing anything in the world right now, what would make me happy? Would being on a tropical island paradise with no internet or phone, somewhere where I can disconnect and just have time for myself do it?" The idea sounded fantastic, but I knew it was not feasible as I had many commitments in the next few months. September was the earliest date possible and that was too far away.

Stubbornly, the next day the thought came back into my head – just thinking about it was making me happy and relieved. I opened my calendar and looked at the next few weeks. It was impossible. I had the Annual General Meeting (AGM) in a week and a half; a wedding in two weeks; and another wedding two weeks later.

Yet on Wednesday, the thought was still there. If I worked over the weekend, missed the AGM, cancelled some dinner arrangements and moved the wedding flight by one day to arrive just in time for the pre-wedding, could I make it work? Yes. Now, if my manager approves, I will be flying next Friday.

Suddenly, all I could think about was my 'Selfish' trip. Disconnecting from my ex-boyfriend, work, the house, my father, social pressure and spending time with 'me' was exactly what I needed. I was so excited. But, where shall I go? I called a friend who had travelled alone the year before and within a minute I made my decision: I am going to Bali.

My manager was not happy that I was suggesting missing the AGM, but for the first time in my working career I didn't care. He said he needed to discuss it with our boss and, on Friday at four thirty PM, I received an email saying, "You are good to go."

This has been the best trip of my life and that is the reason why I am writing about it. I left London running away to forget about my ex-boyfriend but instead I found myself. I did not know it at the time, but I was feeling threatened, I lacked trust in myself and I had a big appetite for freedom. I needed to spend time on my own to connect with myself and follow my instincts.

Just to make sure I am not giving the wrong message, I am not suggesting that getting a ticket to Bali is the solution if you are sad or feel lost, but I believe that it is important to spend some time alone to listen to ourselves and learn about what makes us happy.

Dear Blooming Me

The Departure

It is Friday 2nd June 2017, I just left the office and I am on the Tube on my way to my flat. I cannot believe it; I am going to Bali. I am travelling alone, I am leaving my iPhone at home and I am travelling with a bag. What am I doing? I must make sure I don't forget anything as this time I will not be able to rely on anyone. I have prepared a list with all the things I need to pack, and I have printed the flight tickets. I am travelling with just a borrowed bag, old Nokia phone and old digital camera. This is so late nineties, I love it. But I have mixed feelings; I am excited and at the same time scared.

I get home at five thirty and have thirty minutes to pack everything. Why do I always leave everything to the last minute? I pack everything I have on the list and then a few things more. I pack two books: The Alchemist[1] and Bienvenido Dolor[2] (Welcome Pain). But what if I need a third? I have not read a book in over two years and I am now thinking about reading three books in two weeks? Well, just in case, I look at the unread books on my shelf. Which one sounds entertaining? I choose The Ugly Sister[3]. I review the list one more time, turn-off the boiler, lights and switches, put 'Bali is calling' picture on my Facebook profile picture, take a selfie, send it to my family WhatsApp chat, leave the iPhone on the night-side table and close the door. Oh My God, this is happening.

I start walking to Earl's Court Tube station and my first thought is, "What if the Tube stops and I need to order an Uber to Heathrow? How am I going to do it without my iPhone?" But then, "No worries, you will ask someone, or you will find another way, you always do." I keep walking and two minutes later the bag is killing me: this is too heavy, there is no way I can make it to Asia if I can barely make it to Earl's Court. I am so used to my ex carrying my bags that I forgot how heavy they are. Why did I take a bag? Relax, you will find someone to help you.

---

[1] Paulo Coelho, The Alchemist (Thorsons, 1998).
[2] Pilar Sordo, Bienvenido Dolor (Editorial Oceano de México, 2015).
[3] Jane Fallon, The Ugly Sister (Penguin, 2011).

I get to the Tube. When I am on the platform I look at the screen and realise that I don't know what terminal I should go to. I read the boarding pass, but cannot see any indication. Ok, don't panic, you can ask someone for their phone and Google it on the way to the airport. Why am I panicking every five minutes? I travel every other weekend and I feel like this is the first time I have travelled abroad. Relax and read the boarding pass again. Perfect, here it is in small print. Terminal 4.

I jump on the Tube, take out my note book and start writing down all these thoughts. I want to keep a diary; it will be my way of sharing the experience with someone. I really don't know what I am expecting from the trip; I have had no time to plan or think about it. But whatever happens, it is going to be an incredible experience in my life. I know it, I can feel it. My 'Selfish' trip; no rules. I am just going to do whatever I want, at any time I want. Those mixed feelings are right – I am so exhilarated. I am so terrified.

> **Outfit for the trip:**
> Hat from & Other Stories (great acquisition on Monday in between my meetings in Stockholm), military-style t-shirt from Zara, optical glasses from Ollie Quinn, bag – as big and heavy as me – from The North Face (yellow), white beach bag from Zara Home and flat leather sandals from Office.
>
> **Purpose of the trip:**
> Relax, rest, disconnect and be selfish.
>
> **Potential things to think about:**
> - What do I want to achieve in my life: family, work, be alone?
> - Why do I always say that I am good at everything but excellent at nothing? Where is this feeling coming from?
> - What are the goals that I really want to achieve in the short term?
> - Why do I have to set deadlines for everything? What is the rush?

I'm still at Boston Manor and I don't know what time it is. I don't have a watch or a mobile. I have six Tube stops to get to Terminal 4, Qatar Airlines. Then Doha and, finally, Bali. Total travelling time is twenty-seven hours. Poor me and my bag. I really hope this teaches me how to travel light. I really hope I don't become a hippie, though. I must remember to catch my flight back. My friend is getting married on the 17th of June and she will kill me if I am not there. Also, I cannot quit my job because I have a mortgage. Don't forget.

***

On the plane. Bali here I come! I get a sad feeling because I'm travelling alone, but quickly remember, this is my first adventure. Anything can happen. I just need to make sure that every time I get a thought about my ex-boyfriend I change it immediately into a thought about something else. This is my Selfish trip. But what's that smell? I think it's someone's feet – disgusting.

I start reading the Lonely Planet[4] to decide what I want to do in Bali. I don't even know how many hours this flight will take. The feet smell is extremely strong.

After what turns out to be nearly seven hours, two movies, a quick flick of the Lonely Planet and a small nap, I land in Doha, Qatar. I have eleven hours before my next flight. I look for the Qatar Airlines tour desk and I get my one-day visa stamp and a pass for a free tour around the city.

It is seven in the morning and my tour is not until eleven; meeting time ten AM. I walk around the airport and see some computers. I am not in Bali yet so logging in to do some research on Bali and to check Facebook is not really cheating on my plan to get away from everything.

I open Facebook and have several messages on my Bali profile picture, but only reply to one. My friend Wesley is asking, "When are you going?" I quickly answer, "I'm on my way; I'm at flight connections in Doha." He replies within a second asking if I am travelling alone and I tell him that I need some time off to think. The next thing he writes is, "Gio and I are buying tickets to Bali and we will arrive on Thursday." At the same time Gio messages that I should choose where I would like the three of us to spend the weekend.

The moment I read their messages I start crying. I am so fortunate.

***

---

[4] Lonely Planet, Bali & Lombok. (Lonely Planet, 2015).

I met Gio and Wes seven years ago. When I first moved to London from Hong Kong in April 2010, Wes was the boyfriend of a friend of mine. A friendly Irish boy, always with a smile on his face. Wes used to get out of bed at around eleven PM to eat a digestive biscuit while I was watching 'Sex and the City' in the living room.

Wes, trying to play cupid, introduced me to his friend Gio. However, my thought on Gio was, "Typical cocky Italian who thinks the world moves around his belly!" I did not even try to be nice to him. But he was Wes' best friend, so I met him a second and three hundred other times, and what can I say, Gio is one of those special people who even though they are a pain, it is a pain that you do not want to get rid of.

Time has passed and the three of us have gone through so many things together: Wes' breakup with his girlfriend, her pregnancy with another man, Gio's breakup with his girlfriend, Gio's solo travelling to find himself, my mum and my health issues, my break-ups, etc.

Gio and Wes both moved to Hong Kong two years ago, and I no longer see them so often. But it doesn't matter how much time passes or how far away we are, we are always here for each other. And this time was no different. They didn't ask me if I was ok or if I would like them to visit me in Bali. They just booked a ticket. They were taking a five-hour flight to spend two days with me because they knew I was sad and they wanted to be there for me.

***

Back in Doha airport, I spend the next two hours researching what to do in Bali: I will start with the trip in Canggu (I have already booked two nights), then I will stay in Ubud from Tuesday to Friday and I will meet the boys at Padang Bay to take the boat to the Gili Islands on Friday morning. We can spend the weekend in Gili T or Gili Air and then I will take the ferry back on Sunday to the south of the island, where I will stay until Thursday when I fly back to London. The plan sounds amazing! I take some notes on what to do in Canggu and Ubud and I decide that I will use the boys' phone to do some research on what to do during the second week.

Must do in Canggu:
- Visit Tanah Lot, close to sunset time
- Pantai Batu Bolong Street for coffee: Warung Dandelion (looks like Alice in Wonderland), Crate (at least 1 breakfast there!)
- Canggu traditional market or Pasor Canggu
- Yoga: Desa Seni
- Top spas: Goldust Beauty Lounge and Body Temple

Must do in Ubud:
- Monkey Forest
- Tegallalong rice terraces
- Puri Saren Royal Palace
- Tegenungan Waterfall
- Trek: Mount Batur/Agung
- Rafting: Ayung River
- Eco tour: rice fields. Green Village
- Dinner at Swept Away at the Samaya
- Ubud Water Palace, Saraswati Temple
- Yoga Barn
- Visit a healer: Tjokorda Gde Rai
- Where to stay: Bliss Bungalow

It is nearly ten, so I go back to the tour desk to start my tour. We are a group of around twenty people, but sadly no good-looking men.

The tour is by bus. It is over forty degrees so we all appreciate seeing the city with air conditioning. The bus drives us around and the tour guide highlights the key buildings, which are mainly hotels.

We stop at the Doha market. The heat is crushing and there are not many people on the street. It is Ramadan, so we are advised not to drink or eat in the street as it is very disrespectful. I feel uncomfortable walking around the market by myself. There are only men and they don't have the friendliest faces. I think that my ex should be here with me but then I kill the thought by repeating his words, "I do not love you. I do not miss you." So, no, he should not be here with me. I see two women from the tour and I decide to join them.

The older woman is called Dorma and she is travelling with her cousin's wife, Flora. They are both Filipino, but they live in Melbourne. Dorma has been in Melbourne for over forty years. Travelling was her dream when she was younger. She always wanted to be an 'air hostess' and travel around the world, but her family never allowed it. It reminds me of the time I wanted to be a waitress, and my father didn't allow me. Now that Dorma has no responsibilities she flies all the time.

We talk about her next trips – Victoria and Tasmania in Australia and then Russia. I tell her that my brother Antonio (we call him Tony) and his girlfriend are now on a holiday in the Philippines. Very cheekily Dorma asks me if I hope for Tony's girlfriend to be my future sister-in-law. I smile. I cannot wait for Tony to propose but, while I am the impatient one in the family, he takes years to make decisions. So, I just reply, "I hope so."

Dorma goes quiet and then says, "There are two types of men in this world: the ones who know they want to marry you the moment they meet you, and the ones that hesitate. If he hesitates, leave him." The moment she says that, I feel tears falling behind my sunglasses. I find myself explaining that my ex-boyfriend and I just broke up for that exact same reason. I tell her that I wanted him to move in with me as I felt it was the next step in our relationship and a way to commit to each other but, although he had initially agreed to it, and seemed excited about the idea, he decided to break up because he said he could not see a future together. And I repeat his words in my mind, "I do not love you, I do not want to have kids and I am not sure I want to move in with you." Dorma goes quiet again and I change the topic. I dry my tears and try to focus on the new topic. She is so nice and looks so wise. Maybe this is a sign that breaking up was the right thing and I need to move on.

Back on the bus to the airport, I am so tired I struggle to stay awake. As we say goodbye, Dorma gives me a hug and says, "Only marry someone who loves you, especially if he loves you more than you love him." Again, is this a sign that I must move on? What about the feeling I have that our story together is not over?

***

I met my ex-boyfriend Seb in April 2015. I had double booked myself that weekend, so I spent Friday to Sunday in Barcelona at a hen party and then flew to Amsterdam to go to Kings' Day, the celebrations of King Willem Alexander's birthday.

The plan in Amsterdam was to spend the day in a boat on the canal with fifty people, of whom I only knew one girl. Everyone at the hen tried to convince me not to go to Amsterdam, but there was something inside me that wanted to go. And after all, what is the worst thing that could happen? If I did not like anyone, I could always go back to the hotel or walk around the city. And anyway, how unlucky could I be to not like any of the fifty people?

I landed in Amsterdam on Sunday evening, went to the hotel, changed into my running gear and went for a run. Had a nice shower and texted my friend. We agreed to meet at a bar in an hour.

When I got there, there was no phone connection, so I decided to wait for an hour and, if I could not find her, I would go back to the hotel. The bar and the street were completely packed, but I remember feeling very chilled that I would find her.

My friend appeared within ten minutes and introduced me to so many people I could not even remember all the faces. Except one. It sounds like a movie, but suddenly a face appeared from the bottom between other people and said, "Hi, I'm Seb." I smiled at him and my mind said, "He is the one." I laughed at myself as he could not be the one. He has ginger hair with freckles. I like men with dark hair and big eyebrows. Plus, that only happens in movies. We talked for a bit and, small world, I work with his best friend: different teams, but same company.

I joined the others who wanted to find a 'coffee shop', although they were all closed, and we ended up dancing at the bar. I quickly connected with the group and, despite having a great time, I had another thought about Seb; I kind of wished he was there dancing with us. I disregarded the thought as again, he is ginger with freckles, and I was not looking for a boyfriend.

The next day we all met to take a boat around the canal. When I got to the meeting point, I joined the group. Seb sat next to us in the boat. He started asking me the same questions as the night before. I could not help laughing. It is one of the things about not drinking; you remember everything but the other person doesn't. We didn't talk much more in the boat, but I could feel that he liked me as I caught him looking at me a few times.

When the boat finished, I realised that Seb was waiting for me. We walked together to the restaurant. I cannot remember what we talked about, but I remember feeling very comfortable with him and thinking that he was kind. I enjoyed his company, but I didn't have the desire to flirt with him.

When we got to the park where the others were, we joined different groups. I was chatting to some people in a circle and Seb walked straight up to me and handed me his iPhone. I was surprised but totally loved his confidence. I gave him my phone number and, after that, there is not much to tell. We spent the rest of the day with the group and he didn't make any further move, so I thought that he was probably not that interested.

Seb texted me the next day, just after I landed back in London. Then we chatted during the week, but I could not tell if he was just being friendly or if he was interested in getting to know me better. So, I invited him to a paintball day I had organised with some friends for the following weekend.

Paintballing turned into a barbeque and then into an after party that lasted until five in the morning. That night Seb and I kissed for the first time. I still giggle remembering how he kissed my head and I reacted by kissing his chest. What can I say? He is very tall so his chest was all I could reach. Minutes later we kissed and he said some wonderful things to me that night. Just thinking about that moment makes me smile.

For the next two years, Seb and I grew together. We learnt to complement each other, we were just focused on making each other happy and we became a team. I had my issues that I had to fight and get over and he was also working on his issues because we both wanted to make it work. I was truly myself with him and he made me so happy. I knew he was the one and there could never be enough time to spend with him.

However, after two years I wanted to move forward in the relationship. We planned to move in together in February after my flat was refurbished and, although I think I pushed him into the decision at first, he was keen. At least he was until we realised that I wanted to have kids and he didn't.

We had one or two conversations about the kids but while he got stuck with that, what I really wanted to understand was whether he wanted a future with me. My decision was clear. I wanted to spend the rest of my days with him, with or without kids. He was not clear.

He has never loved anyone, despite being five years in a relationship, and he has always told me that he will only say 'I love you' to the person he will marry.

Although he has never said the words, I have always felt he did love me but just didn't know it. However, one evening at the pub behind my flat it became clear that I was mistaken when he looked me in the eyes and with a cold face said, "I do not love you, I do not want to have kids and I am not sure I want to move in with you." He also said that he would like to get there, that I still had a lot to learn about him and that he was not ready. But it did not matter. What else could he say? He had already said it all. He did not love me. And this time, I believed him.

Hearing those words made me feel very insecure about the relationship and, from then onwards, our relationship went downhill. I felt I was fighting a losing battle because it was now clear in my mind that he did not love me. Even though I tried hard, I could not forget those words. I didn't trust him and I needed him to work with me to find a solution to gain the trust back. But instead he made the decision for both of us, and ended the relationship. He decided that our lives would be happier if we went separate ways.

***

Although I try not to think about Seb, I spend the flight from Doha to Bali crying. I really hope that this trip helps me to forget about 'us'. I have great memories from our two years together, but I have to move on. I need to put myself first. Our 'S&A' Team does not exist anymore, and I need to build new memories, without him.

I think it is hard to move on because I am confused. I really don't understand why he broke up. The way I see it, it is really hard to meet someone with whom you connect, you laugh and, most importantly, you feel comfortable. These two years have been incredible, and I just don't understand how someone can give all that up.

I must accept that there is nothing I can do. I have done nothing wrong. He is the one who has the problem; he is too scared to love, to open himself up and to fight for us. He is the one who quit, so my hands are tied.

Bizarrely, I have something inside me saying that Seb will come back. But I do have to move on. I cannot stop my life to wait for him.

Day 1: Sunday – Bali

The plane just landed. I am in Bali, but I do not feel any different. I leave the plane and join the queue to pass through passport security. The queue is extremely long. I spend an hour until I finally get to pick up my bag. I am not very excited; in fact, I am a bit sad and lonely. What am I going to do in eleven days by myself?

I go to the ATM to get some cash, but the machine says that I should contact my bank. I go to the next ATM and I get the same error message. At the third ATM I get more of the same. Great beginning! I am in Bali with £5 pounds in my wallet and a card that does not give me any cash. I panic for a minute and then I remember that some cash machines don't give cash to European cards, but they accept payments.

I look for a private car hire that does indeed accept card payments and, after talking to the three rental shops and bargaining from four hundred thousand rupiah (twenty-one pounds) to two hundred and fifty (thirteen pounds), I find a driver. His English is good, so I ask him all the typical questions. He is twenty-five years old and is from a city two-hours away from the airport. He would love to travel around the world, but he doesn't do it because he is scared that if he quits his job he will not have a new one when he comes back. He makes three million rupiah (circa one hundred and sixty pounds) per month and he spends half of it on rent. After a bit, I ask him if it is ok if I take a nap. I am tired from the trip and lying down would feel good.

The driver wakes me up when we get to the guest house. I check the room and it looks clean; no luxuries, but it has all I need. In fact, it is quite cute. I leave my bag, take a shower and book a massage for six thirty PM.

The owner of the guest house welcomes me and asks me about my plans during my stay in Canggu. His name is Nyoman and he looks nineteen years old but is forty-one with two children. I would love to know his secret. He is so nice to me that he quickly makes me feel welcome in the country.

I tell Nyoman my plan for that afternoon: I am going to secure my booking for the massage and then am going to Eco Beach. I ask him if he rents mopeds, but the price he offers is double what the guidebook mentions, so I ask him for directions to walk to the main street. Very kindly, he offers me a ride.

Nyoman takes me to his moped, but he has no helmets. I am a bit sceptical at first, but he tells me not to worry. I jump on the back and, as soon as we leave the main entrance of the guest house, it hits me: I am in Bali travelling by myself!

And suddenly I get a gust of emotions: My eyes are wide open to see better, my nose is wide open to smell better and my ears are wide open to hear better. I want to capture everything around me. I feel free, I feel relief, and I feel happy. I think I have made the right decision coming here. Canggu is exactly how I expected Bali to be: hectares of green garden and tropical flowers. It is underdeveloped, but people look happy, friendly and trust-worthy. It is full of organic and healthy restaurants. This might be exactly what I need.

On the way to the village I negotiate the scooter rental with Nyoman. He agrees to offer me a good price only when I mention that I own a Vespa back in London. So, we drive back to the guest house to drop Nyoman off and collect a helmet for me. Just in case, I also ask him for a business card of the guest house. It might come in handy later.

On my way out to the beach, I see a man on the left side of the main entrance. I smile at him and he smiles back. I tell myself, "I am going to be happy."

I start driving. I am alone, and I can do anything I want. I don't need to justify myself to anyone. I don't need to pretend to be happy or to hide if I am sad. I am free. I breathe in. I look around at the houses, at the green, at the people. I smile at every person I see.

I try to memorise the turns as I will need to remember them when I drive back. It feels amazing to just open my eyes and take the place in, instead of having my head in Google maps. I like stopping to ask people for directions to get to the beach.

When I get to Eco Beach, there are many mopeds parked. It surprises me that some have helmets on the handlebars. I wonder if I should leave mine too, but, just in case, I prefer to take it with me – so not fully acclimatised, still a bit of big city London distrust in me.

The sand is black and, although the beach looks nice, Spanish beaches need not be envious. I sound like my father.

I start walking to the right towards an area full of sun loungers. I stop at the first one I see. I look around and I notice how calm it is. There are a few people who look like surfers. I observe the people who walk in front of me and what's noticeable is that every single one of them has tattoos.

There is a guy behind me, he looks handsome, but he is not my type. He is blonde and is reading a very thick book. He looks European and is definitely travelling alone. Although I'm quite happy with my decision to travel alone, I still have some prejudices about it. It's hard for me to accept that I'm on my own, so I guess it comforts me seeing other people doing it too.

I take my book of The Ugly Sister and start reading it until I fall asleep. It is hot, and it feels so relaxing being at the beach listening to the waves, the wind and just resting. I sleep peacefully until a wave reaches my sunbed and takes my flip-flops.

It takes me a few seconds to realise what is happening and, just when I'm thinking that I'm going to drive back shoeless, I see a little kid fishing my shoes from the water. I smile broadly. Balinese people seem so happy, friendly, helpful and generous. Why is it so different in London?

The sea is rising, so the woman from the bar suggests I move to another sunbed. The first one I see is the one behind me, next to the guy who looked like another solo traveller. I sit next to him and open my book.

I think I manage to read one paragraph before he asks me about my book. This might be how solo travellers engage with people, so I close my book and accept his offer of conversation.

His name is Patrick. He is thirty-four years old and German. He tells me that he travels alone quite often. His mum died of a stroke and after that, he went travelling to heal. He felt that travelling helped him put things into perspective. Years later, his father remarried, and his step mum got cancer. He went travelling before her chemo treatment to gather the strength to support her. When she passed away he became very sad and went into a dark space. Until his best friend died in an accident, which made him realise that life is too short to be sad and that being happy is a choice. Since then, he travels as much as he can. He works a few months first to make some money and then spends it travelling.

It grips my attention when he mentions that he wants to be 'normal', but I keep quiet as I don't really know what to say. I want to ask, "What is normal?" because my father always says, "Normal is now the abnormal." I agree with Dad. The way I see it is that normal does not exist because people have no boundaries anymore and therefore I think he should do whatever makes him happy, at the same time as making sure that he respects others. But I am not certain where this comment could take us, so I keep the thoughts to myself.

We keep talking about life and I realise that during the last few weeks I have been complaining that life is so unfair and asking why everything happens to me when I am actually very lucky. Yes, during the last few years all my family have had serious medical problems, but we are all alive and healthy and I should be grateful for that. Patrick has lost his mother, his step mother and his best friend. Life is hard for everybody. We all go through difficult moments and lose people on the way, people who are important to us. But it is part of our life and we need to learn how to accept it and live with it.

I decide to tell him about my mother.

***

Mum had her second stroke in February 2013. It was my second week in a new job when my brother called me and said, "Mum just had a stroke and I am not sure you are going to make it on time." I was paralysed. For a second my mind refused to believe it and I felt nothing. I called my boyfriend at the time; I needed to tell someone to process what was going on. But the moment I said the words, I had to hang up and run to my computer to buy the next ticket home to the north of Spain.

I grabbed my handbag and ran to the airport. I remember that trip as a dark tunnel. I was completely drained and couldn't stop crying. The feeling of anxiety was like knives cutting my stomach and I needed to feel that pain to be able to exteriorise the psychological pain I was feeling. I could only think that she must not leave me; we still had so many things to live together. She is my companion. She simply was not allowed to leave me just yet.

I called my father when I got to the airport. He was in Madrid because he had some business meetings and was, like me, waiting for the next flight to get home. We were both in shock. We could not talk, we had nothing to say to each other, but it felt good to have him on the other side of the phone. I think he needed me too.

Doctors said that, in her condition, she would be gone within three days, but even if she managed to get through those three days, she would be unable to do anything for herself. Three days later she was still in a coma. The consultant told my father that it would have been better if she had not made it.

Tony, my brother, was devastated. I remember that first night as if it was yesterday. He woke up in the middle of the night and could not stop shaking. He was scared that he was going to lose her without telling her how much he loved her. That night I told myself I had to be strong for him. I thought that if he saw that I was not sad and looked at the situation in a positive way, it would give him the strength to do the same. Unfortunately, he did not see it that way. He thought that I was being unrealistic and felt that I was not supporting him.

Dad was relying on faith. It was all he was saying. The first night we went back home, Dad asked us if we wanted to sleep with him in the same bedroom. Tony said no, and I just followed him. Tony and I slept in Tony's room and Dad slept alone. Four years later, I still regret my decision. We should have spent the night as a family. If I could go back in time, I would persuade my brother to stay together. We all needed it.

And me, I could not feel anything. I could not take what the doctors were saying because that would mean I was giving up on my mother, and so, when I saw my mum move her foot on the second day I took that as a sign that she was going to recover. No-one else saw her moving her feet but I did not care; my mum made that move to tell me not to give up because she was going to be ok.

Those months were the worst months of my life. Tony could not understand that I did not want to listen to the doctors who were preparing us for the worst; Dad and Tony were arguing about the best treatment options, and I was going with the flow. I could not make any decision. I was working in London during the week and sleeping at the hospital over the weekend. When I was in London I felt lost, sad and alone; when I was in the hospital with mum I felt useless, sad and lost.

My family fell apart in the process. We did not understand each other, and we did not know how to support each other. Tony was always complaining about me: I was not there for him; I was not spending enough time with Mum. He even said he was ashamed of having me as a sister. I was travelling home as much as I could. I was working extra hours during the week to compensate for leaving early on Fridays – I suggested quitting my job. But nothing was good enough. I felt that no matter what I did, it was never good enough for Tony.

Mum was in a coma for twenty days. But she recovered. Doctors said she would only improve for the first nine months, but, four years later, she keeps improving. She has some secondary effects, which are only noticeable when you spend some time with her. But, she is an independent woman who walks, drives, dances, sings and cooks. Dad had a huge impact on her recovery. She is a fighter and the combination of Dad's determination to help her become independent, and her own strength and perseverance have been the key to her successful recovery.

***

Talking to Patrick reminds me of how lucky I am and how silly I have been lately – being sad for missing my 'old' Mum when I should be happy because I can still see her laughing.

I also mention to Patrick about my operation, but he looks so shocked that I decide not to go into details. We change the subject. It is getting a bit awkward to talk about such deep topics with someone I barely know. I don't even know why we started talking about it in the first place.

A few minutes later my alarm rings. It is time to get a massage. I say goodbye to Patrick and head out.

While I walk to the moped, I look around. Between sleeping, reading and talking to Patrick I have not properly enjoyed the place. The sea is beautiful and there are people still surfing. More people have arrived and the bar area is full. The sun is setting and there is a live band playing Bob Marley's 'No woman no cry'. I smile.

***

One-hour massage. It was really good, but I am still not fully relaxed. As I don't feel like going back to the guest house just yet, I walk around the little stores and restaurants. Although it is already dark, there is light and music coming from everywhere. I take a few pictures, but I don't really know what else to do, so I take the moped and drive back home.

On the way back, I drive slowly enjoying the view, the wind and the vibe of the village. I feel happy; it is as if I have stopped time and left all my problems in London. Finally, I'm starting to feel relaxed.

As expected, I struggle to find the entrance of the guest house. I manage to drive to the street, but there is no sign to help me find the main entrance. I don't worry. Although there is no light in the street, I feel safe and know I will find it. I just don't know how long it is going to take.

In the middle of the street, I stop at a store where there are some locals. They don't speak English, but somehow they give me directions when I hand them the guest house business card. It takes three more attempts until I find it, but eventually I get home safe and sound. It is ten PM; I will sleep for ten hours and have breakfast at eight AM.

Dear Blooming Me

Day 2: Monday – Canggu

I open one eye and feel the sun coming inside the room through the curtains. It's going to be a sunny day and I am going to get tanned! What time is it? I'm sure it is still early and I can stay in bed five more minutes.

I look at my Nokia and, oh my God, it's one PM! I have slept nearly sixteen hours! I have not slept this long since I worked in investment banking. I am rested though. No five minutes more, it's time to wake up, get a shower and head to Finns Beach Club.

Back on my moped. It feels good to drive around; this place is so beautiful. Again, I drive slowly, savouring every view and every corner. I stop at Crate for brunch.

I look at the people; all look so relaxed and young. Most of them look like surfers and this time eighty percent of them have tattoos. I start thinking that tattoos and surfing skills are prerequisites to being a tourist in Bali.

Dear Blooming Me

I drive on to Finns Beach Club, once more asking for directions every five meters to make sure I don't get lost. You have to trust that the people you ask understand what you are saying and that they are offering you the right direction. This is hard to believe when every time you get the same answer, "Straight and right." I always wonder, what right? The first one, the second one… I try to pay attention to every corner to make sure I learn the way back; this place is quite far from my guest house.

Twenty minutes later, I get to Finns Beach Club. It is very trendy. It reminds me of the typical European beach club: Blue Marlin in Ibiza or Nemo in Mykonos. I am a bit disappointed as this is not what I was looking for on this holiday. Even so I can't deny that the place is superb. I get a sunbed and order a smoothie. I totally see myself here with my friends, ordering mojitos and having the best time. There is a DJ on a platform over the swimming pool – great music, beautiful people and fantastic weather. Like in Blue Marlin, the sea is at the end of the club and there is no beach, just water.

I call Gio to get some details on their Thursday flight. He was worried because he had not heard from me since I was in Doha, two days ago. My first thought is, "Maybe Seb is also worried?" I am such an idiot. This is not about Seb; it is about me. I immediately delete the thought and focus on the fact that he does not want to spend his life with me. The longer it takes me to accept it, the more painful it will be, and the longer it will take me to get over it.

Gio and Wes will arrive late on Thursday night and we'll go to the Gili Islands together on Friday. I am in charge of getting the boat tickets as it is easier to do it from here. I open my notebook and add it to my to-do list: Three tickets from Padang Bai to Gili Air. Meeting Gio and Wes on Friday at one PM at the pier.

I open my book, The Ugly Sister, which is quite entertaining. It tells the story of two sisters, one very pretty and the other, not ugly but with a normal beauty. The sisters stop all contact when the pretty one is 'discovered' and transformed into a successful, well-known model. Twenty years later, they try to reconnect but instead of spending time together, the former model goes to the gym, spa or auditions while using her sister to take her nieces around town. The sister, unsurprisingly, ends up feeling like the hired help.

I try to relax and read, but I cannot concentrate on the book. My mind will not stop. I cannot stop thinking about the best strategy to forget about Seb. I have been strong in real, difficult moments in my life, so why am I being weak now?

I have always thought that my way of protecting myself was to pretend that things were not happening. But I am realising that I was just dealing with the present as it comes. When there is nothing in my power that can influence events, I just rely on faith.

This is what I should do right now. I have to accept that Seb and I are not together and simply wish for the best to come. I have to find what makes me happy and I have to start putting my needs ahead of the needs of others. This reminds me of my list of things to think about during the trip; I need to focus on why I think I am good at everything but excellent at nothing. This is my new challenge: get to know myself.

I psychoanalyse myself for a bit longer, until I decide it is enough. I need a massage, so I book an appointment in thirty minutes time. I grab my belongings and ask for the bill. When it comes, I learn that there is a minimum spend and so I decide to come back for dinner. There are worse places to eat.

On the road again, this time I ask for directions at least five times before I get to the massage place, thankfully on time. Prices are expensive for Bali, but I'm already there and, after all, it is still cheap in comparison to London.

The massage is alright, but I find once more that I cannot fully relax. I don't understand what is wrong with me; massages are my favourite thing in the world and lately I have not totally enjoyed them.

I drive back to Finns Beach Club but surprisingly, or maybe not, I get lost. I stop a guy on a moped who takes his phone out and drives me to the club using Google Maps. That is cheating.

Finns, apart from the DJ and some people drinking and dancing in the swimming pool, is empty. There is one single guy sitting on a puff chair by the pool next to where I sit. I open my book and order dinner.

Music in the background and a view to the sea and the stars. I am enjoying my solo time. So, when the single guy tries to engage in a conversation, I cut him off straight away. Also, I get the impression, by the way he approaches me, that there is a chance he will have a few more beers and will try to make a move on me, which would be awkward. So, very politely, I tell him I am reading my book. I feel bad for ignoring him but I don't feel like talking to him, and this trip is all about me and what I want.

Dinner, dessert and two peppermint teas later, I realise that it's already eleven PM. It's dark outside and I don't know how to get back to my guest house. What can I do? Basically, I have two options: get lost and take an hour to get back to the hotel or get a taxi and follow it with the moped. I decide to go for the second option. I really don't want to spend an hour driving in the middle of nowhere trying my luck.

While I'm driving behind the scooter taxi, I realise that I'm completely vulnerable. The driver is a woman who works for the beach club and she is taking me through short cuts I don't know. She could be taking me home, or she could just as easily be taking me to the middle of nowhere to relieve me of wallet and passport. But, for some reason I feel safe. I trust her totally and, in fact, it feels amazing to drive at night concentrating on the view, the smell and the unique atmosphere.

When I get to the guest house, Nyoman is waiting for me at the main door. The taxi driver had called him to ask for directions. He suggests that I call him next time to pick me up instead of paying a taxi. He is so sweet.

I go to bed, but I cannot fall asleep. I try all the tricks: day dream, count sheep and focus on the inside of my eyes. Not being able to sleep is bad enough, but even worse is that I am not sure whether the reason I cannot sleep is the jet lag, the sixteen hours I slept the previous night, or Seb. I feel like I'm between the devil who says that I have to move on because Seb has made his decision and is never coming back, and the angel who wants me to listen to my instincts telling me that he will come back.

But why do I have this feeling that our story is not over yet, that he needs time to sort his fears and that he will come back? I strongly believe in my instincts because they have proven to be right in the past; I cannot explain how it works, but I can only say that it does. However, I am scared that I'm only fooling myself. Surely, I have to move on.

Dear Blooming Me

Day 3: Tuesday – Canggu / Ubud

The guest house makes a delicious omelette with toast and tea for breakfast. Today is my last day in Canggu so I chill for a bit at the pool. Nyoman drives me to an ATM to get some cash out and offers to drive me to Ubud for three hundred rupiah.

I say goodbye to the staff and get into Nyoman's car. I am expecting to see an old car but instead, he appears with a new white 4x4 with incorporated GPS. Bali keeps surprising me. There are many things on this island that are undeveloped, and at the same time, there are many similarities to the western world.

On the way to Ubud we talk a bit about everything and Nyoman teaches me some Balinese words. Nyoman asks me to add him on Facebook with his android. It is so tempting to open my Facebook and my Gmail. I try to log in to Gmail, but he hasn't taught me those words, so I take it as a sign that I should not open it.

The trip to Ubud only takes forty-five minutes and we get there before I realise it. Five minutes before arriving, Gio texts me to check on the boat tickets. I stress for a bit. I like being efficient and I didn't like to say that I had not started to look into it.

As soon as we get to my hotel, using a number recommended by the ever helpful Nyoman, I ring the boat ticket guy and bargain him down from one million two hundred rupiah to nine hundred rupiah for a return trip including commute. I think it's a great deal, but I tell him that I need to check with my friends first.

Gio, who never trusts anyone he hasn't met, starts complaining that I'm being ripped off and that I should talk to another friend who was in Bali a few weeks ago. I go back to the guy and manage to negotiate him down to five hundred rupiah. Gio is still complaining. Now he says that the price is too cheap and that they are ripping me off. I really don't want to stress for a boat ticket, so I text Gio: "This is the price I got. It's booked for Friday. If you find something better, call the guy and cancel." Gio notices that he is upsetting me, so he apologises and says that he hopes we are not going to end up without a boat. I breathe in and breathe out.

I give a big hug to Nyoman and thank him for all his help.

**

The hotel in Ubud looks beautiful. It's exactly what you expect in Bali: masses of vegetation and small canals between the footpaths. The rooms are small houses and they are surrounded by a rice plantation. I have booked a superior room, so when I check in the first question I get is, "Is it just you?" I want to scream, "Yes, my boyfriend just broke up with me!" But instead, I smile and say, "Yes, it's just me, thank you."

I take the key and the bellboy walks me to my room. When he opens the door, I am over the moon; the room is so pretty. I want to share my enthusiasm, but I am alone, so the best thing I can do is to give myself a silent hi-five. But that immediately makes me feel immensely lonely. This is the moment I realise that I don't like travelling alone. This trip is what I needed, but I like sharing and not being able to share these moments with anybody is annoying.

The hotel has a spa area where I book a massage for tonight before heading down town. The hotel, at around a thirty-minute walk, is a bit far from the city centre, but it is lovely strolling through the streets with the locals. Many ask, "Taxi?"

I stop everywhere that calls my attention. A beautiful temple that is closed, but the garden surroundings are breath-taking. I see a lot of vegetation through a door and I enter to see it more closely; I follow the stairs, which take me to a spa. I really like this city. It has so many things and it's so charming and creative. There are funny billboards everywhere. One coffee shop has a board that says, "We have Wi-Fi so you can sit down and ignore each other."

I walk all the way down to the Monkey Forest. The moment I'm buying the ticket I think: "I'm doing this because it's one of the Must Do's, but do I really want to see monkeys?" I walk around in a very speedy way, although I have to admit that the monkeys are quite a fun attraction for tourists and kids.

I keep walking around the city. There are so many stores with beautiful things. Thank goodness I cannot fit anything else in my bag, otherwise I would buy loads. Suddenly, I see a restaurant called Three Monkeys: it has umbrellas, a view and peace – perfect.

Usually I don't like eating alone in a restaurant. In fact, if I have to eat alone, I prefer to get a sandwich to take away. But today I am relaxed and enjoying my book. The 'ugly' sister has fallen in love with her sister's husband and fakes having a relationship with a friend to hide her feelings. But on top of all the romantic drama, the two sisters get into a fight and Abi (the 'ugly' one) admits to Cleo (the model) that she was jealous of how often their parents talked about her and how highly they praised her. To Abi's surprise, Cleo admits that she was always talking about her beauty because her parents so often highlighted how proud they were of Abi, her smartness and path to University. Basically, the book is about sibling rivalry.

It suddenly hits me. I have never realised it, but now it makes sense; that feeling that I am good at everything but not excellent at anything is because I have always compared myself to my brother. That is also why I used to say that I was the black sheep of the family.

***

Tony is eight years older than me and he is the perfect son every parent wants to have. He is smart, sweet and responsible. He is an engineer, speaks four languages and has built his own company.

When I was a child, I remember that all I wanted was his attention. I would follow him everywhere; whether he was playing videogames, watching the Ninja Turtles or going out with his friends, I wanted to be there. The problem was that the age gap was too big and so I would not usually be part of his plan. But I didn't care – I was always ready for the next time that he would ask me to join him.

I would do any activity he liked doing, and my goal would be to be good at it so it would be fun for Tony to do it with me. This dynamic made me become very competitive.

Tony moved to Madrid to go to university when I was only nine years old. During my teens I was raised hearing how perfect Tony was. All my parents could talk about was how proud they were of him.

I didn't like it. Tony was a teenager and, when he did come home, playing with his little sister was not exciting for him. He preferred to meet his friends or do his own things. My parents had not seen their child for months and wanted to spend as much time as possible with him. It makes perfect sense to me now, but back then it made me very jealous and I focused all my energies on trying to be better than Tony in order to make them proud and focus on me. The problem is that I would try to be better at the things that Tony was excellent at, and these were things where all I could be was good. I never realised that he was always better than me, not because I was not excellent but because he was older, more experienced and it was an activity that he had chosen.

There are so many examples that come easily and clearly to mind. One of them was volleyball. Tony played volleyball and he was so good that he went to regionals. I played volleyball in school even though my group of friends were the basketball team. I was very good. I was the captain of the team, but I never made it to regionals because I was not tall enough. I still remember how sad I was when my coach gave me the bad news.

> *Suddenly I realise that the problem is not that Tony is excellent and I am not. The problem is that I tend to devalue myself by paying no attention to my achievements and focusing on the areas where I have to improve. It is the same thing that my dad used to do when I gave him my grades: if I got an A he would say, "It is your job!" but if I got a B he would say, "You need to aim for an A!" I never got recognition for exceeding, so today, I only focus on the things I need to improve.*

This also makes me think I live for others. I set my goals to make my parents or my friends feel proud of me. But does it make me happy? I keep looking for challenges to exceed and hear people saying that I am extraordinary. But when is it going to be enough?

***

I have a chocolate brownie to compensate for a healthy dinner, pay the bill and walk to Yoga Barn. I want to get some information about the classes. Then I get a scooter taxi back to the hotel. I have a massage booked at eight PM and I want to make sure I'm there on time.

I negotiate the price for the taxi with a man, but his daughter is the one who drives me to the hotel. She looks no older than fifteen. I ask for a helmet and she gives me hers. I don't know what to do or say, so I just put it on and say thanks. She drives me through all the short cuts and I realise that I had taken the longest path to get to the Monkey Forest. She asks me the typical questions of where I am from and if I like Bali. She is overweight and scruffy, but she has a very sweet look.

When we get to the hotel, I get off the scooter and give her a bill of fifty thousand rupiah. Although I negotiated forty thousand, I want her to keep the extra ten thousand for herself. She opens her eyes and her face shines, "For me?" It totally made my day.

Later that night, I try to fall asleep but the neighbours, Germans I think, are making too much noise. They don't stop talking and laughing, and it seems as if they are opening and closing doors – repeatedly and with some force. I try to ignore it, but it is nearly one in the morning. After trying to fall asleep for an hour, I decide to ask them to keep quiet. I really don't like complaining to neighbours, but it was unbearable.

Back in my room, sleep is still impossible as I cannot shut my mind off. I turn on the light and take my note book and start writing what my mind tells me. It is trying to decide what I want to do next.

Work:
- Change company? Higher salary, higher rank, more responsibility
- Regain passion for what I do. Enjoy as I enjoyed working in my first job in Mergers and Acquisitions
- City? I don't know. I want chance or destiny to choose. Definitely not Spain

Exam:
- Take the Chartered Alternative Investment Analyst exam? Not sure I want to do it

Flat:
- Complete the lease extension
- Learn about neighbour harassment law. The neighbour is driving me crazy and I need to find a way to get her to stop. She complains about everything
- Buy a house

Gym:
- Go back and create a routine
- Start and finish Kayla training
- Get firm legs so they don't shake when I dance
- EAT HEALTHILY, no chocolate!

Boyfriend:
- Someone who loves me and wants to take care of me – I used to take this one for granted
- Someone who wants to make a team with me
- Someone who wants to build a future with me
- Obviously, I need to want/have the above for him too

Other:
- Voluntary experience abroad?
- Travel for a month (or more) with a boyfriend
- I want to find the one and be relaxed that I found him and just enjoy the time with him
- I want to have a family. Kids? I like the idea of having a family but not sure if I'm ready to take care of kids yet
- Marriage? I like the concept of gathering all my family and friends to tell them that I have made the decision to share the rest of my life with someone, but I don't really need a paper signed by the state or the church

Day 4: Wednesday – Ubud

There are so many places to visit in Ubud and it's already ten AM. On second thoughts, there is no rush. Let's have breakfast and decide what to do.

I decide to spend the morning by the swimming pool finishing The Ugly Sister. The swimming pool is secluded from the hotel rooms and it is surrounded by an enormous variety of exotic plants.

There is just one other person there, who is also reading. There is no noise; the only noise you can hear is coming from a fountain, which pours water into the swimming pool. The sun is not very strong, which makes it the perfect place to enjoy the reading.

After finishing the book, – which brings the expected endings: one happy, one sad – I decide to head back to town. Like the day before, I walk and many locals ask, "Taxi?"

Once in town, I stop at an internet café – it has been years since I've seen one of these. I open my Gmail and my Facebook accounts and I get quite sad when I see that I have no news from Seb. This brings a big negative mood, which takes over the rest of the afternoon.

He might not be the one. He is not coming back. He is stubborn and if he has made a decision, he is not going to change his mind. He has never loved anyone and if he has not been able to love me in two years, he will never do it. "You are not the exception here; you are the rule." But this is not the way I should approach it – I need to understand how I feel about it.

I feel betrayed. I feel I shared everything with him and he did not open himself to me. I feel like I have lived a different relationship from him. It is not possible that someone who has lived the last two years wants to give it up.

But why did I feel he was the one? I have two sides: the one that does not want to give up and wants to have faith; and the one that does not want to be fooled again and wants to focus on the words he said, "I do not love you, I do not want to have kids and I am not sure I want to move in with you." But why am I so determined to have hope when it is so clear that there is none?

I stop at a coffee shop because I need a break from my own mind. The coffee shop is very rustic. Everything is made of wood and there are two types of tables: normal tables with four chairs, and tables with bed mats where you can lie down. The back of the restaurant is open and the view is towards a small rice plantation. It's beautiful. I sit down on one of the bed mats and order a watermelon juice.

I grab my next book from my handbag and realise that I've brought the wrong one. I wanted to read Bienvenido Dolor by Pilar Sordo and I've got The Alchemist by Paulo Coelho.

I think about starting to read The Alchemist, but I just don't feel like it. I get the feeling that I should read it next week.

With no book to read, I open my travelling notebook and start thinking about words that have had an impact on my life:

Friends:
- You have to listen more and talk less
- You think you are the main character of your own movie
- Maybe you should focus on your personal life rather than your work life because when you get older you could end up alone
- Studying was never your thing
- You are not girlfriend material
- So and so says that you treat me badly

Family:
- I am ashamed of having you as a sister, you are so selfish
- You are a brat and have no say here

Work:
- Your work exceeds expectations, but I must rank you with meets expectations because you are too direct and come across as aggressive

I get interrupted by Wayan, the tour guy who is organising a night hiking tour of Mount Batur. He is calling me to meet up to arrange for the payment for the tour I have booked for that night.

I'm hungry, so I move to a restaurant across the road to have some pizza. I think it's time to stop self-psychoanalysing, so I open The Alchemist. But it's no good – after three pages I feel bored. I clearly don't want to read this book today. I decide to look for a bookstore on the way back to the hotel so I can read something entertaining that night; I have no plans and the hotel spa is fully booked.

On my way, spotting a bookstore, I go in. After looking around I see a book called Born to Love, Cursed to Feel[5] and it seems so relevant to my state that I think, "Interesting, it might be a sign." The blurb on the back just says, "I will carry you wherever you need to go." This is definitely a sign. I buy the book and walk back to the hotel, excited to start reading my new book.

***

I meet Wayan when I get to the hotel and he greets me with a big hug. In no rush, we sit and decide on my itinerary for the next day – two tours: night hiking on Mount Batur from two AM to ten AM, followed by rice fields from ten AM to four PM. We take a few selfies and then say goodbye.

I am very excited about going on a tour. I have been two days without talking for long to anyone. I really think I have been punished for not talking to the single guy at Finns Beach Club.

I get to my room and start reading my new book. Where is it going to take me or, actually, where do I want it to take me? Hopefully it will give me some clarity.

I start reading the first page and am horrified. This book is not for me. When I read it I feel like the writer has lost the purpose of her life because she has been dumped. I have been dumped too but I don't share any of the feelings that are being described. I get a pen to highlight some messages that could be useful for me but, even though I am trying really hard to identify myself with those sentences, I struggle.

---

[5] Samantha King, Born to Love, Cursed to Feel (Andrews McMeel Publishing, 2016).

The book helps me realise that, although I miss Seb and I can't understand his reasons for breaking up, I do not need him in my life in order for me to be happy. I am one of the luckiest people I know: I have the best family in the world, and top friends who are always there for me; I am healthy and I have a good job to maintain my lifestyle. Yes, I would like to build a future with someone, but only if I meet the right person.

I give up on the book and get into bed. This book is taking me nowhere.

I try to fall asleep but, again, I cannot shut down my mind, which is going over and over the same thoughts to the point that I am becoming angry with myself for allowing the circles.

I realise there is no way this is going to stop until I properly analyse it, and so I turn on the light and get my notebook.

List of what I do not like about Seb:
- Lack of affection and love
- He did not want to build a future together or have a family
- Incapable of opening himself up either emotionally or personally
- He will not make me feel I am the most important person in the world
- He does not apologise
- He makes decisions on his own
- He is too cold; sometimes it feels like he has no feelings
- He is a quitter/coward for giving up on us so quickly
- He does not want commitment
- […]
- He does not miss me or us

I read all I have written and I surprise myself. I really didn't know the list was so long. I actually thought there was nothing that bothered me about him. But these are pretty serious things. Why did I not realise it before? And if these things are true, why am I still hung up on him? Am I hung up on him because I love him, or is it because I don't want to give up on him because I felt he was the one when I met him?

Either / or, I still love him.

Day 5: Thursday – Ubud

I manage to rest an hour or so, then at one AM I hear the alarm. I have no idea if a van, a car or a bus is picking me up or even if someone will show up at all. But what I know for sure is that if no one comes in thirty minutes, I am going back to sleep.

And then I see a van and get excited. But it's not mine. Five minutes later my van appears and it's full of people. This is promising; I'm so bored of just talking to myself that I find I'm quite keen to meet some people. I look around to see who is going to be my victim, but it is too dark, and I'm too tired. I close my eyes and try to sleep.

The van takes us to a hotel and the driver tells us to sit in the cafeteria area. I'm walking next to some people, but they don't seem that interesting, so I slow my pace to check who is coming next. They are two men; tall and handsome. I just found my targets.

I let them pick a table and I sit in front of them and introduce myself. They are Spanish too. From that moment at two AM in the night until ten in the morning we don't stop talking.

Fernando and Agustin are from Cadiz, the south of Spain. We talk about the usual: our trip, Bali, travelling experiences. Agustin and I do most of the talking, Fernando is on WhatsApp. We get some tea and a single biscuit, and we get back to the van.

On the way to the mountain we are the only ones talking in the van; people must hate us. At the start point of the hike our guide gives us a lantern, although mine is probably from a cheap store because the light is minimal. We start walking. Agustin goes first, me and then Fernando. We try to engage with the guide but there is no chance. Her English is limited, and she just says "Yes". You can imagine how many jokes we get out of that.

We walk for four or five hours until we reach the summit. I don't know when, but at some point, we stop asking questions about each other and just start bantering. It feels like we have known each other for years. We are a team of three. Agustin takes his plastic poncho for the rain and puts it on the floor. They look at me and say, "The girl in the middle." We share their snacks, take pictures, record a video with my old Nokia and laugh at everything we say. I like their company and they like mine. I feel like I have regained my confidence, which I didn't realised I'd lost. I feel happy and I can tell that I am shining.

Unfortunately, we are not that lucky with the weather. The sky is cloudy, which hides the view and so we start descending the mountain. It takes us longer than expected and Wayan phones me a couple of times to see how I'm getting on. He is trying to sort the logistics to pick me up to join the rice plantation tour. I'm all sweaty and would love to have a shower and a nap, but I still go straight on to the next tour. Although I'm tired, I'm also excited. It is the first day of the trip that I feel this way. It is also the first day have something to do.

Having an active day full of plans makes me realise that this is me. I enjoy being busy and making plans; I like meeting new people, doing activities and trying new things. Also, spending time with Agustin and Fernando makes me remember that people like spending time with me and being my friend.

When the tour finishes, the driver takes the group back to their hotels and leaves me at the coffee shop where I'm meeting Wayan. I give a big hug to Agustin and Fernando and we exchange phone details in case we can meet for dinner later.

The coffee place is breath-taking. It's an outdoor terrace with a huge rice field; you cannot see the end of it. When I get there, Wayan introduces me to the two girls who will join me on the tour – I quickly get their story. They are both South African, 26 years old and currently living in London, which is where they met and became friends. They are now travelling around Bali for two weeks.

We walk around the rice plantation and the temples inside. Wayan tells us all about the temples, the traditions, the myths and the rice collection process. He talks so much and so quickly that it is hard to follow. But he is focused on helping us get the best experience of Ubud. I really like him.

After a couple of hours, we agree that we have seen enough, and we go to see the Tegenungan Waterfall. It's a scenic waterfall in a lush jungle setting, above a shallow bathing area. There are some cafes nearby where you can see the waterfall and we go there to take some pictures. We don't need to get any closer. After a few shots, we decide it's time to finish the tour and drive back to Ubud.

I'm exhausted and cannot wait to get to the hotel. Even Wayan is surprised that I'm still awake. He keeps saying that I'm a machine. But when we are getting closer to Ubud I change my mind: it is my last day in Ubud and if I don't go to Yoga Barn today, it is unlikely I will come back. Yoga Barn is the most famous yoga place in Bali and every person I know has recommended it to me. I cannot miss it.

The next class is in an hour. So, I have dinner at a restaurant next to the yoga centre before the session starts. I am starving; I have not eaten anything today.

I think about my parents; I want to hear Mum's voice. I need to hear her saying that everything is going to be fine. I call home and Dad picks up the phone. He is so happy to hear from me, but then there is something in his voice that annoys me: he is worried about me.

I know it is normal that parents worry about their children. However, my goal in life is to make my father proud. If he is worried about me, it makes me feel weak.

***

I have always seen a family as the father being the president and the mother the CEO. The president is the one who has the final say and the one who makes the final decisions. However, the CEO manages the company.

Mum was the one who would pick me up from school to take me to English, ballet or any other extra activity I had. She would take me shopping, she would study with me, and would hug me when I cried.

My father has always been very strict with my brother and me – the same way his father was with him. He has taught us to work hard and to be ambitious. Thanks to him, we are both successful.

Growing up, my conversations with Dad were about grades, work and money. I shared my feelings with Mum and aimed to make Dad proud. And, although this dynamic has changed with age, and I like sharing with Dad many more stories now, I do not like Dad to think that I am weak. I want him to see me strong, unbeatable, successful and happy.

Since Seb and I broke up, Dad has been worried about me. He checks on me more frequently and he tells me that he loves me at the end of every sentence. Seeing him worry makes me think that I am not ok and I put pressure on myself to be happy, when what I need is some time to process my feelings.

I am also angry because I am going through a stage in which I prefer to minimise any contact with Dad because I need to find myself and define what makes me happy. He has such a big influence on me that I question whether my ideas and goals are mine or his. Anything he says has a massive impact: if he says I need to save x amount of money, I don't stop until I do; if he says he would like me to buy a flat, I don't stop until I buy it. I didn't realise just how big was the impact of his words until, a few months back, he said that marriage is not important, and I started to think that I don't need to get married.

***

I talk to Dad for a couple of minutes and when he is going to give the phone to Mum I run out of credit on the phone. It is a shame; I want to hear her voice. I need her to say that everything is going to be ok, that I am going to be ok.

At Yoga Barn I find the reception area and buy a ticket for the next class. As I'm still a bit early, I look around to kill some time and walk to the room. I try to open the door but when I pull it, it doesn't open. I look at the woman who is next to me and she laughs. It's a sliding door. I laugh with her at my stupidity and we start talking until the class starts.

Her name is Ramona and she is from Germany. She is thirty-five years old and has been married for eleven years. Her husband divorced her a year and a half ago, and she realised that maybe she was not that in love with him because it didn't take her long to fall in love again. However, the new guy didn't want to commit, so it ended after a few months. Since then, she has been feeling empty and so she has given herself a sabbatical travelling to find herself.

"Why are you in Bali?" is the first question that Ramona asks me. And to my surprise I reply, "My boyfriend broke up with me because he doesn't love me." Why am I telling this to a stranger? And, in seconds, tears star falling down my cheeks.

I am so ashamed of myself. The previous night I had decided that it was enough; I don't want to be with someone who is afraid to love. Then why am I crying? With a peaceful face, she smiles at me and says, "Don't worry, it's normal. You need to ask yourself how you feel about the situation." I smile at her. This is what my psychologist has been telling me for the last few weeks.

The class is about to start so I dry my tears and we go inside the room. The teacher has a hippie look and gives me a very good vibe. His name is Leo. I am chilled, so I just follow what he says without thinking much. I'm not sure if it is because I'm tired or if it is the combination of the music and the slow movements with Leo's words, but I feel relieved. My body has no tensions, and for the first time, I feel that my mind is quiet. It feels good. I have taken a few yoga classes before, but this has definitely been the best one I have ever attended.

Ramona and I are chatting outside when a guy joins our conversation. We start talking about the weather, but we end up talking about our failing relationships. We are such a cliché: we are in Bali, in Yoga Barn, to find ourselves because we are heartbroken.

We talk about the classes at Yoga Barn and both of them mention a Shamanic breathing class they attended the day before. Ramona looks at me and tells me I should definitely try it. She says it will be useful for me and I will like it.

The guy leaves and Ramona and I keep talking for a bit. She teases me that there was some attraction between me and the guy and I laugh: I am not ready yet.

I really like Ramona. She is so calm, she comforts me. And most importantly, I feel like she doesn't judge anything I say. I want to spend more time with her to learn about her findings during her travels. Maybe I will come back to Ubud before leaving.

Dear Blooming Me

We talk about the classes of yoga that we be have taken without a feature or breathing exercise and the day calms. Karma is to get the shit out, the Taste is leftover in it. Since you will be useful by you, it will like.

The guidance is I feel me comfort to talk to long it. She teases a satisfied to me about other life between us, and the curving breath is new all it Yes.

Firmly she told me, she hurt certain to cost it says. "I am wondering". I am thinking once under my "and I am a typewriter. I will let is happy about it form. Remember it move for it I will give I added. "Hate takes such to.

Day 6: Friday – Gili

I have made so many plans for Friday morning. Instead, I wake up at ten fifteen, rush to the shower, fill my bag with all my belongings and make the bus driver wait fifteen minutes. Today is the day I'm meeting Gio and Wes!

Gio calls me desperately about ten times because the bus has not picked them up and they have been waiting for more than an hour. He keeps telling me I have been ripped off until I tell him that my van has arrived on time. I don't want to argue because I am so excited that I'm going to see the boys. I try to calm Gio down. Gio is not Gio if he does not complain – it's part of his charm.

After over an hour driving, the van stops in a street that is full of cars and trucks. It's the only road to the pier so there is nothing we can do other than wait. We wait for forty-five minutes until a guy comes and tells us that we have to walk one kilometre to the pier, otherwise we'll miss our ferry. There is no way I can walk a kilometre with my bag, so I ask for help and the guy that came to tell us to walk offers to carry my bag. I feel such a spoiled girl because the man is my height and probably skinnier than me, but I'm relieved because I would cry if I had to carry it.

Eventually, we get to the agency and ten minutes later the boys appear. Gio is smiling but Wesley is grumpy – this is something I have never seen before. He is grumpy because the Balinese's chilled culture stresses him out. He likes punctuality – chaos and disorder drive him mad.

It's so fantastic to see them and, at the same time, I feel they have made such a big trip for me that I must make this the best weekend of their lives. But this feeling only lasts five minutes. I'm with family.

Being with Gio and Wes, I feel protected. Once more they are unconditionally there for me and they are never going to let me down. It does not matter where we are in the world, if I need them, they will be there for me and I will be there for them. I remember when I called Gio two and a half years ago telling him I was going to have an operation. He only asked, "When?" "Monday, tenth of November," I replied and immediately he came back with, "We will be there on Friday." I remember trying to convince him to come later on so that I could show them the city. But he didn't give me an option, he just said, "We land on Friday." They were there for me then, and they are here for me now.

They are the best friends in the world.

***

Gili Air looks very calm and quiet. Many locals are offering to take us to the hotel by horse, but we decide to walk. Poor boys, they are carrying my bag. I try to bargain about the horses, but the boys insist on walking, and we head to Captain Coconut Hostel.

We walk for ten minutes until we get to the entrance of the hostel. I am really happy when we get there and I see that it doesn't look like a hostel. The entrance has a bar on the left and some tables on the right. The decoration is simple and vintage. Behind the bar is the swimming pool with a few sunbeds. At the front are some dorms, and at the left is the villa, where we'll be staying.

Our villa is amazing. It has a 'shabby chic' style. The boys decide to share one room and I take the other one. We leave our stuff and jump into the swimming pool.

The one other girl in the swimming pool looks at us. It's funny because now that I have been travelling alone, I can easily spot solo travellers. She is looking around with open eyes trying to identify people to talk to.

Sure enough, within seconds she starts talking to us. She tells us that she has been travelling for months and is now approaching the end of her trip. She talks about some of her experiences and the countries she has visited. We ask her what she liked the most and she mentions trekking to Mount Rinjani, an active volcano, in Lombok. I think that it sounds really cool; it's a three days/two nights trek. But, as I'm not very into trekking and don't have many left days, I don't think about it any further. However, I have to admit this triggers something in my mind. If one of her favourite places on her travels between Australasia and South East Asia is in Lombok, the island next door which is just thirty minutes away, shouldn't I go?

Wes and I keep asking her questions and Gio uses every opportunity to mention that he has also done a sabbatical and how much experience he has as a solo traveller.

***

Wes and I go to see the sunset. We stop at a bar on the beach that has colourful puff chairs. There is chilled music playing in the background and people are having drinks while enjoying the sunset. The sky is red and it is very peaceful. We sit at one of the sunbeds and order a pizza, a beer and a watermelon juice.

Wes asks me about Seb. I can see he is worried about me. I tell him the story and how confused I am. Like me, Wes doesn't understand how Seb could change his mind so quickly from being so happy in the relationship to breaking up. Wes gives me his take: Seb probably has some issues, but he recommends that I shouldn't waste my time trying to work out why it didn't work. He says I should focus on myself and focus on doing new activities. Time puts things in proper perspective and, if we are meant to be together, he will come back, but I should not stop my life and wait for him.

I like hearing Wes' opinion. He has a way of looking at things from a simple and logical perspective, removing any type of drama. It sounds so easy and so logical when he says it that I can only agree. I feel he totally understands my frustration, but Wes and I have always had a similar approach to relationships.

We try to analyse it a bit further but there is not much more to say. Plus, Gio joins us and takes over the conversation. When he hears that we are talking about Seb, he makes it very clear: I have to move on. He says I should not make the same mistake he made when he hoped that his girlfriend would come back to him.

Gio met his ex-girlfriend five years ago on a trip he made to Argentina. He felt sparks as soon as he saw her and fell for her immediately. She lived in Argentina and he was living in London at the time. They had a long-distance relationship for a year and a week before she was due to move to London she broke up with him. They are still in contact and, apparently, he is still waiting for her to tell him that they should get back together.

We change the topic now as we really feel we've said all we can. We are hungry so we have dinner at a restaurant next door. It has a barbeque and we order a bit of everything to share between the three. We talk about Wes' ex-girlfriend as we always do. Despite the fact that she hasn't hung out with us for a long time, we all care about her even though she has let all of us down on several occasions.

She is an important part of our lives. Without her we wouldn't have met each other, but, as Wes points out, it's the three of us who always make an effort to be there for each other. We may not know each other's birthdays by heart but if any of us is in need, we will be there.

We have a few drinks and three chocolate ice-cream desserts. We spend hours talking about nothing, just enjoying our company and calling up silly memories. Then we walk back to the hostel.

This is the first night I fall asleep peacefully.

Dear Blooming Me

Day 7: Saturday – Gili

I open one eye and I can hear the boys walking around the villa. I wake up, we have breakfast and we go to explore the island.

We rent pedal bikes but park them half way through; there is so much sand that we cannot cycle. Instead, we walk. With Gio complaining all the way, Wes playing with his drone, and me talking, this is just like old times.

The island is very small, so in less than an hour we are back to the hostel. While relaxing at the swimming pool, we meet a Swiss guy from Bern. He looks in his early twenties, but he is in his early thirties. He just quit his job and is travelling before he starts the new one. He has been with his girlfriend for eight years and when he goes back to Europe will travel in a caravan with her around Scotland. He is going to do his diving induction in Gili and then is going to do the same three-day trek in Lombok as the British girl we met at the swimming pool the day before. I wonder again if I should do the trek. But I disregard the thought; three days is too long.

Later in the afternoon, we walk to pick up the pedal bikes and stop to get some ice cream on the way back. When we get back to the hostel it is sunset, so we go to the bar with the puff chairs. Wes wants to play a bit more with his drone, Gio orders a beer and I start thinking about the volcano trek. Should I take the chance? How many times am I going to have the opportunity to hike an active volcano? Do I have enough time to then catch the plane?

I think about the different options; I would like to go to the south of the island and go back to Ubud to take the class that Ramona recommended on Wednesday. If I leave at seven AM tomorrow and make sure I take the three PM boat on Tuesday, I could go to the south of the island, visit it in the evening and get back to Ubud just in time for the class.

I discuss it with Gio and he agrees it's a good idea. So, before I change my mind, I go to talk to the different organisers. I cycle store by store asking for prices, which range between one million two hundred and one million five hundred rupiah. I manage to get the one million two hundred and, just before I give them the deposit, I decide to wait. I want to discuss it with the boys during dinner. I feel bad for leaving earlier and not spending the morning with them. They have travelled all the way to Bali just to be with me.

Wesley tells me not to be silly and encourages me to do it, saying he would do it if he was me. I know it sounds crazy, but I also think the trek is a great idea. I am doing what I feel like and, weirdly, I feel strongly that I should not miss this experience.

On the way to dinner we return the bikes and I pay for my trip. I need to be ready for seven in the morning.

Day 8: Sunday – Lombok

Wes knocks on my door at six fifteen to say goodbye; he is going to see the sunrise with his drone. I wish I was as diligent as he is; I would have given up on the sunrise the minute the alarm rang. We say goodbye and I give him a great big hug. I am going to miss him.

Once I'm ready, I go to Gio's room to wake him up. He is sleeping peacefully.

I feel awful waking him, and especially bad asking him to walk me to the pier, but I cannot carry my bag. As expected, I get a, "For God's sake, Amadora!", which is his usual complaining sentence. Every time I think about him saying that it makes me smile. We walk to the pier and we see Wes playing with his drone. He looks as happy as a five-year-old with a new toy. I am going to miss them both, terribly.

We stop at the place where I bought the tickets the night before and some guys help me carry the bag to the pier. I give Gio a big hug. I really don't want to leave the boys, but I'm also very excited about going to Lombok to trek the volcano. I have been a week in Bali, have four days left and I'm determined to make the best of them.

I wait for ten minutes before the boat arrives. The boat is the one you have probably seen in documentaries, islanders use it for their commute between islands. In fact, most of the people in the boat are Indonesians.

A half Portuguese / half Australian man offers to carry my bag inside the boat. I follow him and his girlfriend and I ask them all sort of questions during our trip to Lombok. He is Portuguese but raised in Melbourne and she is Austrian but has lived in Thailand for the last four years. They are traveling before moving to Cascais, a town next to Lisbon (Portugal), where he is planning to open his own Pilates centre. She is quite scared about moving to Cascais and does not look very keen about it.

The boat trip to Lombok takes less than twenty minutes. When we get off the boat, I give them my email address so they can send me their details to forward to my Portuguese friends once they open their Pilates centre. We say goodbye at the pier and I hear a guy shouting "Amanda." That must be me! I follow him and another couple who have also been in the boat. I think we are going to do the same tour.

***

We clean our feet before jumping into a car where there are two other girls. This is going to be my trekking team: Chelsea and Kelly, and Leticia and Philipe. Chelsea and Kelly are both American, and are friends from University. Kelly is travelling for eight months because she doesn't know what to do; she has been travelling since quitting an unfulfilling job. Chelsea works for an association that helps problematic kids to study and get a career. Leticia and Philipe are Brazilians living in New York and are currently finalising their visas to move to Australia. He is a physiotherapist, and she is a writer and a movie producer. She went travelling in Thailand, Vietnam and Cambodia three years ago, wrote a book about her experience and used crowdfunding to make a movie of the book.

We are all so excited about trekking and meeting each other. We don't stop talking. They all seem super lovely. This is going to be fun.

The van takes us to an outdoor room full of tables and some locals offer us some tea/coffee and banana pancakes. The banana pancakes are delicious!

After breakfast, the tour guys lend me a smaller backpack and my bag goes into storage. I realise I am not very prepared for this trip when I pack my pyjamas and face cleaning products (which I quickly remove), but I will manage.

We jump into a van that drives us for fifteen minutes with a local guy who is going to trek the volcano with us. We cannot pronounce his name, so he suggests we call him Gadi. His English is not very good, but he is laughing all the time and so we become fond of him very quickly. He is missing half of his teeth.

We start walking up Mt Rinjani and it seems easy, but we soon discover that it is harder than it looks. In less than an hour we are all covered in sweat. Leticia and Philipe lead, Kelly follows and then Chelsea and me. Gadi is behind me smiling with his half teeth and cheering us up to keep going. He is carrying all of our stuff: food, tents and sleeping bags. He has two baskets joined by a stick, which he has slung over one shoulder, the baskets dangling front and back. He is wearing flip-flops and moves as quickly as a fox.

Chelsea starts asking me questions about my job. I explain to her that I do private equity fund investments for an asset manager – we raise money from financial institutions and wealthy people and then invest it in funds that invest in companies. She asks me what I like most about my job and what I like least. I tell her that I really like the fact that I can use both my analytical and social skills: analysing company performance and fund performance at the same time as engaging with fund managers to develop good relationships and understand more about their investment strategy. However, what I don't like is that the organisation has grown so much that I am now in a hierarchy where I have little decision-making control over what I can do. I realise I deeply miss the old entrepreneurial culture in the firm. I also tell her about how much my approach to work has changed in the last few years. While I used to have a big passion for what I do when I was working in investment banking, the years have been swift to make me more bonus-oriented. I still care about learning, but my goal is to increase my total compensation at the end of the year. The moment I say that I feel ashamed of myself. It is sad to say, but it is true.

Chelsea tells me about her job. She works for an organisation that helps different schools in the US. When someone starts working with the organisation they don't know the school or the state they are going to be working with – it could just as easily be New York as it could be New Orleans.

She is a manager and designs the program for the students at her school, the purpose of which is to identify some kids who need help, and then work with them to develop their ambition and career potential. This entails everything from providing advice on their careers to offering psychological support.

She talks about how beautiful it is to see kids who have gone through the program come back to work with the organisation to support other kids with similar backgrounds. It gives a strong message to the children, not least that if they work hard, it will make a difference.

> *Listening to Chelsea talk about her job and why she does it makes me feel even less impressed with what I do and even more embarrassed by my previous comment on the bonus. It makes me realise how important it is to be happy and proud of what you do. Working hard used to be my main priority and I used to be happy spending hours at the office working on projects. I would feel fulfilled. Now, however, my priorities have changed. Now, the most important thing for me is to spend quality time with the people I love and make them feel how special they are for me.*

We make our first stop and Gadi introduces us to four guys and a girl who make up our group. We are so tired that we can only say hi to them. They do the same. We also meet the rest of the porters and our guide.

We sit on the grass to eat. We keep chatting among ourselves about what we do, what we like and what we would like to do in the future.

Meanwhile, Gadi feeds us. He brings us biscuits, tea and noodle soup. I have to admit that if I were not on a mountain, I would never have started to eat the soup, even if I had to starve. But he brings it with such a big smile that my thoughts of, "Is this clean?" and "I have not washed my hands," are quickly dispelled. I am so grateful, and in fact, the food is delicious.

I notice that Chelsea has a tattoo that says, "Hope springs eternal." In general, I am very curious to know the stories behind tattoos. Some people don't like talking about them, preferring to keep them secret; however, people who do tell allow you to learn a lot about them.

This time was no different. When Chelsea was sixteen, she became paralysed. For months, she was unable to walk or move and was fully dependent on her mum. She had multiple sclerosis and all the doctors she met at the time told her that there was nothing much that they or anybody could do. However, she never gave up and kept talking to different doctors. She could do something – she had Hope.

When, months later, she recovered her ability to walk, she got a tattoo on her foot to remember the importance of Hope. Unfortunately, this disease does not disappear and she had another episode when she was at university. She was leaving the bathroom in her dorm when she fell down and once again she could not move. Her friends panicked because they did not know what to do. Neither did she.

But today, Chelsea is trekking a volcano with me. She says that she is aware that one day she will not be able to walk again but, in the meantime, she is doing all she can to make the best out of her life and to do as much exercise as she can to help delay the disease.

I am so impressed. It makes me think about how important it is to never give up. If you really want something, you should have faith that it will happen and never, never give up. Things take time and patience. It is all about having a positive attitude.

We walk for seven hours to the volcano. There are some areas, especially at the end, that are very challenging and we have to walk on our hands and knees to make sure we don't fall. However, we dare not complain when the porters are carrying all our stuff in bare feet or flip-flops and still they smile.

People descending the mountain keep saying, "Good luck" and, although we sort of appreciate the motivation, those words don't help at all.

The weather, never very good, starts raining when we get near the crater of the volcano. The porters set up all the tents and, although we try to help, we slow them down and decide it is better to let them do it alone.

Chelsea, Kelly and I retreat into one of the tents and eat all their snacks as we gossip about previous boyfriends, school stories, etc. I feel like in a summer camp. Unfortunately, the weather doesn't improve so helpful Gadi brings our dinner to the tent. He is so kind.

It is eight PM and we are so tired that we decide to go to bed. I leave the American girls and go over to the tent I'm sharing with the girl from the other group: Canadian, travelling for a bit before returning to Canada to start working. She tells me that when she was younger she lived in Thailand with a host family. I'm surprised by her country selection; I have always seen international exchanges as an opportunity to learn English or French – how euro-centric of me. Of course, it makes sense to go to get new cultural experiences too and also learn other languages such as Thai.

But we don't talk for long as we are very tired. The Canadian girl falls asleep very quickly but I struggle. I am lying too close to the tent cover and the rain and the wind keep waking me up. It is freezing cold. I try to move but the Canadian girl is in the middle of the tent and I don't want to wake her up. Also, I'm using my backpack as a pillow trying not to think about how dirty it is, or about how many people have slept in that sleeping bag.

I start thinking about Seb. I have not had any thoughts about him or us for a few days, but that night everything comes back. This is so frustrating. I cannot wait for the night to be over. I always knew that camping was not my accommodation of preference but tonight, I can certainly confirm it. I will see the volcano in the morning but will not go further up the mountain. Instead, I will descend the mountain. I would prefer not to see the summit than spend another night like this.

Day 9: Monday – Lombok / Uluwatu

Last night was horrendous and I feel tired today. I absolutely don't need to spend another night in these conditions. I want to brush my teeth and have a nice warm shower. Clean sheets. I came to Bali to relax, not to struggle. My hair is dirty and I can't get out of my head the uncountable others who have slept in this sleeping bag. Yes, I will see the volcano and make the descent today.

Gadi brings us breakfast. Pancakes and hot tea. He is a star! Kelly comes to say goodbye and to exchange phone numbers, but the moment she opens the tent I can hear myself shouting: "Go With Them!" I ask her about the volcano and she says that they might not be able to see it. Oh. I want to descend with them, but I do want to see the volcano otherwise what is the point of going all the way up? I suggest we look for our guide and ask how we can get to the volcano.

He is next to my tent and says that we can see the volcano from a view point that is three hundred metres from us. Kelly and I call Chelsea, and the three of us walk towards the volcano. I cannot believe it has been so close to us and we didn't know it.

The volcano is surrounded by a lake. I am looking at a hidden place; I could look at it for hours. It is the most beautiful view I have ever seen. It is stunning. It is totally worth going all the way up.

I take a memory picture and the girls take some real ones, and then we go down the mountain.

I want to take the three PM boat to Bali and the girls need to take their boat at four PM. We better keep going.

Although the girls are chatting a lot about different things, I am detached; the bad night seems to have triggered something. I get immersed in my thoughts: what I want, what I do not want, Seb, work, house, future, age. There is no decision I can make from the mountain, but it feels good to think and worry about it.

Many people are walking up the hill and we try to give them motivational speeches such as: "It is totally worth it," "You are going to love the view." Obviously, we avoid the self-satisfied 'Good luck'.

My legs start weakening and I nearly fall on a few occasions. I am tired and my stomach is very upset, probably from the lack of hygiene. But I am keen to reach the bottom as soon as possible. I do not want to miss my boat. I cannot wait to have a warm shower.

We realise that we have lost our porter. He was with another girl descending the mountain, but they were walking at a slower pace. We have no idea how we are going to get back to base: we don't have the phone number of the agency; the girls don't have international minutes and my Nokia battery is flat. But I tell the girls not to worry; this is Bali where everything gets done and things always work out. They agree, so we decide to worry when we get to the bottom.

Which we do in about four hours. But none of us gets much reaction, we just take a picture. We are more concerned about how we are going to get to base. There are some locals and we ask them if they know our guide and, to our surprise, they do. Very kindly, one of them calls the agency who instructs us to go down a bit further where then they will pick us up.

We do as we are told but we forget to ask for the phone number of the agency in case we cannot find them. We walk until we get to where the van left us the day before. What can we do now? How long do we have to wait? Who is going to pick us up? We have no idea. But again, I am not worried. I am convinced that everything is going to be ok and we will find our driver.

There is a small store on the road. A very old woman is seated outside. She introduces herself and invites us inside the store. It is really hot outside, so it is nice to get in the shade. I ask if she has a charger for my phone, but she doesn't, so we wait.

Without even thinking where I am, I remove my t-shirt leaving just my sports bra on – thankfully, the old lady is so used to the behaviour of stranger westerners that she was unfazed. Kelly asks me about the scar I have on my tummy. It is quite an obvious one as it is over twenty centimetres long. I have no complex about it but I always feel weird explaining it to someone for the first time because no one knows how to react. I guess it is not frequent for people to hear someone say, "I don't have a stomach." They are intrigued and I tell them the story about my stomach cancer.

***

In October 2014, I was feeling very weak and I went to the doctor, who ran some blood tests, which showed I had high levels of anaemia. My anaemia was so high the doctor sent me straight to the hospital to get a blood transfusion.

The hospital doctors said I might have an internal bleed and ordered an Oesophago-Gastro-Duodenoscopy. The test showed that I had three tumours around my stomach. I called Mum and jokingly I told her I had three 'balls' in my stomach but was not worried about it. She told me that this was no joke and that it could be a tumour or cancer. I laughed as this would be impossible and told her not to worry. But when the doctor came back and told me that my best chance would be chemo, I started to cry.

I didn't know how I was going to handle this. I called my ex-boyfriend with whom I had not talked in ages as we had broken up a year earlier. I don't know why I called him first, when I had two good friends waiting for me downstairs, but I needed to calm down before I could call my parents. I didn't want to worry them. I cried it all out and then, I called them.

The doctor did a biopsy and said he would call me with the results. However, a week and a half later, I was still chasing the doctors for some answers and they had none. My friends insisted I flew to Spain to ask for a second opinion. Two of them are doctors and the uncle of one of them is part of the top gastro-enterology team in my region. I flew home and scheduled a meeting with Tino.

Tino ran the tests and told me I had five tumours spread on the top and the bottom of my stomach and the best option was to remove the whole stomach. I remember when he said that my brother looked like he was going to throw up, Dad was about to have a heart attack, and Mum could not talk. My only question was, "Are there any side effects?" Tino played it very smart. He looked at me and explained that this operation is similar to the one to help fat people get thin. The difference in my case was that they would remove the whole stomach. The worst thing that could happen is that I will struggle to gain weight, which is the best news you can give to a woman. That is what I decided to remember. The operation was scheduled for a week later.

My closest friends flew or drove from Madrid to my home town in the north of Spain and we organised a stomach farewell. I was not very aware of what I was going through and, to be honest, I saw no point in over-analysing it. My approach was: I have something in my stomach that is not good and it needs to be removed. Let's do it and get it over with.

The operation was very successful and my recovery was incredible. There were some tough moments, but these I would instantly delete from my mind. In fact, I remember the whole experience as a great time. The doctors and nurses at the hospital made me feel at home and I have no words for my family and friends. I cannot express how much love and support they gave me.

Tony slept with me at the hospital the night before the operation. He sat on a chair next to me the whole night. I loved that he was there with me. Mum was with me every day. I think these days helped us both; it helped her in her recovery because she had to step up as a mother and it helped me to have her by my side. Dad was the one who suffered the most. He was in the hospital twenty-four/seven but he had to be in the guest room because it was too painful for him to see me in the hospital bed.

My auntie came as soon as she could and spent a couple of days with me. My friends organised themselves to make sure there was at least one of them with me every day. They flew from all over to be with me. Who would not make a great recovery under these conditions? The success of my recovery was all thanks to them.

I remember the first weekend after the operation when Gio and Wesley flew from London. The doctor had told me on Thursday that I must walk more, but I was really struggling because it was painful. However, knowing my friends were making such an effort brought me energy. On Friday, I was walking all over the hospital. By Saturday, I was playing Bingo and being so loud that one of my favourite nurses had to tell us off. Four days later, Tino gave me the green light to go home and, in one month and a half, I was back at work. Maybe a bit too soon, but I was very bored at home.

During the whole time I only cried twice: the day the doctor said it could be cancer and one morning during my recovery. I remember I opened my eyes and my head started thinking that I was going to be the weird person who could not go out for dinner and who would never have a boyfriend because no-one would want to be with a person without a stomach. I allowed myself to feel sad for a minute and then I said, "Enough! It is not going to take over your life." And it did not. I started living my day as if it was the last: enjoying every minute of every day, saying yes to every plan and spending every minute with the people I love – my family and my friends.

***

We wait for a bit longer at the store and then decide to say goodbye to the lovely old lady and start walking. We see some cars, but none of them are from our agency. We try calling the company that the girls used to book the trip, but we get nothing out of them. We don't know what else we can do when, suddenly, a van comes and the driver tells us to jump in.

I don't recognise him at first but he is the guy who had asked me if I was a marathon runner the day before. I love this country. You don't know when things are going to happen but you can trust that they will get done. Balinese will always find the way. Maybe it is the cousin of the cousin who knows the neighbour who is probably best friends with the person who you need. I agree with Gio, I totally fit into this culture.

We get to the place where we left our stuff. We are excited about having a warm shower, but when I go to the bathroom the shower head doesn't work. I go for option two: hands, face, armpits, feet and loads of perfume!

Chelsea falls asleep between two chairs, I organise my bag and Kelly chats over her phone. A bit later, I ask Kelly if I can use her phone to text a friend of a friend called Maria. I haven't met her yet but I talked to her when I was still in London and we agreed that I would stay a few days at her place. She lives in Ullwatu, in the south of Bali, and rents one room on Airbnb. When we talked, she sounded like she needed to rent her room to cover all the money she had spent refurbishing the house. Because I told her that I would stay a few days with her, I feel obliged to spend at least one night at her place; although there is something in me saying to go back to Ubud. Still, I decide to go to her area, convincing myself that I will visit the beaches in the south, said to be the most stunning ones of the island.

Twenty minutes later, one of the local guys comes to tell me I have to leave now otherwise I will miss my boat. I say goodbye to Chelsea and Kelly. I make it quick as I don't want to get sentimental. They have been so helpful to me on the trek and I have gotten so very fond of them that I feel sad leaving them.

***

We get to the port three minutes before three PM, the appointed departure time. I was a bit stressed in the car as I was afraid I was going to miss the boat. But once we get to the port I realised that I needn't have worried. I am in Bali and nothing is ever on time.

The boat left at four thirty PM. As I wait for the boat to leave, a tropical rainstorm prompts me to congratulate myself on making the decision to descend the mountain. I would be so upset if I was trekking in the rain.

After walking back and forth for at least half an hour, I decide to sit. I sit next to a girl who I think is one of the most beautiful young girls I have ever seen. She is blonde with aquamarine eyes. We start talking to each other about the potential departure time of the boat, what we have visited in Bali, our lives, and we don't stop chatting until we get to Bali. She is twelve years younger than me but the conversation flows as if we had been friends for years.

Joanna lives in Germany and she is eighteen years old. She dated a guy for four years who cheated on her and when she forgave him, he became jealous and possessive. He got so jealous and possessive that, without her realising it, she was becoming sad and depressed.

Her mother didn't know what to do to help her and asked her ex-husband, Joanna's father, to talk to her. Their relationship was not great, but he was also very worried and wanted to help. He suggested she take the test to become a ski instructor. Joanna likes skiing and liked the idea. The day she passed the exam, her father told her that he was proud of her and that made her world.

Because of her boyfriend, she had lost all trust in herself over the last few years and, now that she was doing something for herself, it was a great feeling. Working as a ski instructor and becoming independent helped her get stronger and make the decision that it was time to break up with her boyfriend.

> *When she says that, I realise how important it is to trust yourself and know what makes you happy. My happiness depends on me and it is a mistake to rely on others to be happy. I have to start doing the things that make me happy instead of the ones I think will make others feel proud of me.*

I tell her about Seb and how I feel that the story is not over, but the reality is that it is over. She says something that is very helpful. She says, "If you love something, let it go. If it comes back to you, it's yours forever. If it doesn't, then it was never meant to be."

The moment she says this it makes sense. Although in previous relationships I have broken up with my partners, I have always contacted them post breakup. This time, although I miss him with all my heart, there is something in me that doesn't want to contact him.

> *I realise that Seb has issues and whatever they are he needs to sort them out. If he is really the one and loves me like I think he does, he will come back. And if he doesn't, it was worth breaking up early, so I could get on with my life.*

Talking about him makes me feel sad, so I suggest changing the subject.

The trip from Lombok to Bali passes by really quickly. I like my chat with Joanna and I am actually impressed by her. She is only eighteen, but she looks so strong, enthusiastic, free and powerful. I would like to learn more about her, but it is already dark and we both have to go. We say goodbye and promise to keep in touch.

***

After nearly two hours in a taxi, I finally meet Maria at a Korean restaurant next to her house. Maria looks younger than I expected. She is forty-three, blonde and, although she is casually dressed, you can tell she is good-looking.

She introduces me to her dog to which she keeps talking, saying, "He is so handsome. He is the best dog! Who loves you?" I don't want to judge her but seeing her talking to him that way makes me think she is a bit crazy.

She asks me if I want to have dinner at the Korean restaurant or if I prefer to go somewhere else. I am quite keen to have pizza, so we go to an Italian restaurant where she knows the manager. The dog, Maria, my eighteen kilogram bag and I jump onto her Vespa.

Maria does all the talking over dinner. She talks about her house issues, her money problems, a new tenant who is coming the next day, how tired she is, etc. The first thirty minutes are ok, but when she goes on and on about all these issues I start to get quite uncomfortable. She seems nice and I feel sorry that she is stressed with all these problems. I try to change the type of conversation and compliment her as I can tell she is the type of person who loves that, but she always finds a way to come back to the same topics.

I suggest having a massage and her eyes light up. I don't want to be mean, but I get the feeling that she is thinking I could shower at the massage shop instead of at her place so then she doesn't have to clean the bathroom for her next guest. I try to ignore the hint but, after my massage, I can't believe it when she actually opens the door of the room to remind me to shower there.

I try to ignore it and remain positive, but the irritations continue. On the way to her house, she tells me that I have to check out before twelve PM, but five minutes later she tells me that I should wake up at nine AM so she can show me where the scooter rental is. Before I can react, she tells me that she is not going to wait for me to wake up and waste her morning. I breathe in and breathe out. This is unbelievable. She is definitely the worst host I have ever met in my life. Thank goodness I hadn't committed to staying with her for the whole ten days.

And to add insult to injury, the room made it difficult to sleep. There are so many noises outside the house. I cannot close the window because it is very hot, and I cannot use the air conditioning because Maria doesn't have any credit left on the electricity.

Day 10: Tuesday – Uluwatu / Ubud

After a fitful night, I wake up in that empty room to the noise of heavy tropical rain. It's not even eight thirty AM yet, so I try to go back to sleep. There is no way I can visit the area and the beaches in this weather.

But sleep is impossible. I get up and organise my hefty bag. I try to charge the phone but there is no electricity. "Luxury house in Bali," I remember Maria saying. I laugh in silence.

At nine AM Maria knocks at my door, tells me she is going to buy electricity and quizzes me about my plan. I ask her if I can use her computer to book a hotel in Ubud, but there is something going on with her computer, so she lends me her phone instead.

She starts going over and over the same things as the previous night: the bad deal that she got with the house, the new guest in the house, money. I cannot believe I have to hear all of this again, especially first thing in the morning. All this repeated negativity about everything is very uncomfortable to me; it seems impossible to change the subject.

She starts tidying my room and takes the towels. I have not had a shower yet and so I ask her to leave them. Her face goes white. I can tell that she is annoyed about having to clean the bathroom, but she cannot complain about it. I am already so irritated with her that I really don't care what she is thinking. I'm going to have a shower.

She finally leaves, and I concentrate on finding a place to stay in Ubud that night. I text Ramona, the German girl I met at Yoga Barn, who is still in Ubud and she gives me the name of her guest house. Thankfully, they have some rooms available. I will stay there.

Maria comes back and I suggest going for breakfast. I want to be polite, which I quickly regret. She says it is raining too hard and does not want to leave the house again. But then she offers to have breakfast at the house, making sure I understand that she is doing me a favour and saving me eighty thousand rupiah. She is such a good host.

She goes on and on about her next guest. First, she hopes he is not intending to spend all the internet credit because then it might not be worth renting him the room. Then, she hopes he will stay for a whole week because if he only stays for two days she will have to change the sheets and clean the room again. I try to change topic by joking that he may make it all worthwhile by his extreme good looks, but she ignores me and we are back to the bad deal she made on the house and how awful the builders were. I want to leave that house.

I need to get a taxi to Ubud but, most of all, I need a break from Maria.

Maria claims not to have the phone number of a cheap taxi driver or the Uber app, so I decide to go to the streets to find one.

As soon as I close the door, I look around and find myself in a dirty street in the middle of nowhere. I feel sad and lonely. I don't know what I'm doing in Uluwatu or in Bali. Why am I alone? Why am I sad? Why is everything so hard?

Maria's negativity has brought me down, but I need to take control of the situation. I need to find a taxi to get out of there. I look around and, although I don't know how or where I am going to find it, I know that I will. I ask at a small food store. No luck there. I walk on and stop at a store that looks like a pharmacy. A man opens the door and asks, "Massage?" "No, thanks. Taxi?" He looks back at me, "Uber?" My eyes open wide, "Yes, please!"

As I wait, all of a sudden, I start crying. It is a mix of all the bad feelings I got from Maria and the fear of becoming a single, forty-three-year-old crazy woman like her. I am scared. I cannot stop crying because I don't want to be alone. At the same time, I am thinking that single women over thirty-five behave very peculiarly and I don't want to become one of them. I know this is irrational, but I can't help being scared by the thought.

The man looks at me and asks what is wrong. I feel so stupid as I tell him that my ex-boyfriend broke up with me because he did not love me. He doesn't know what to do. He's probably thinking I'm crazy. Who asks for a taxi, sits down and starts crying? But I can't stop and I don't want to stop. I'm sad, I don't know what I'm doing here and all I want is to get out of this dirty street and go back to Ubud.

Ten minutes later my Uber arrives. I dry my tears, apologise for all the drama and leave.

I collect my bag at Maria's and say goodbye. I sit in the back of the taxi, open my book Bienvenido Dolor and, without reading a single page, start crying again. What is wrong with me?

Kadek, the driver, asks me what is wrong. Poor him. Another stranger I am going to bore with my first world problems. I tell him that my boyfriend never loved me, and he tries to calm me down by saying that love is the most important thing in the world and I should not be with someone who is not capable of love. I know that his answer is not going to calm me down. My problem is not that Seb does not love me; my real problem is that I feel lonely and I don't understand why my life is so hard. In the last six-months I feel I have been fighting against everything and I don't want to keep fighting alone. Are all the struggles I have been through in the last few years with Mum's stroke and my cancer not enough? The moment I mention my cancer, Kadek changes his speech.

Kadek tells me that I have to pray to be happy and to be strong. He says it does not matter who I pray to, but it is important to pray to have faith. I have already started praying during the trip. Not every day, but a few times. He says I have to do it at least every day because it really works.

He tells me that years ago his wife became seriously ill when she was pregnant with his first son. He was very sad because he could not help her. He didn't have the money to take her to the hospital and he was scared that something bad could happen to her or the baby. He was very down, until one day he started praying. He prayed for days, until one day he was happy. His friends could not understand why he was happy, and he did not know why either, but he was very happy. He knew that things were going to be ok. And they were – his wife is healthy, and he is the father of two children.

We talk all the way to Ubud. I feel so grateful for his time and his words. He takes me to the guest house where Ramona is staying and waits until they confirm that I can stay for the night. I give Kadek a big hug and we agree to meet at nine thirty PM the next day.

I leave my stuff in the room and start walking towards Yoga Barn. I want to go to a yoga class and a meditation class but it is too early. As I walk around it starts raining, so I decide to get a massage nearby. I get a one-hour massage and, just as I am about to pay, I see they have a package offer with a facial, manicure and pedicure. I am in. I sit down, open my book and have four hours of pampering. There is going to be no yoga today.

When I finish I head to the same restaurant, the Three Monkeys, that I went to on my first night. I sit down and order a steak, while I finish reading Bienvenido Dolor. It is the second time I read it, but I really like its message. In particular, I like what it says about life. It says that we all have to go through difficult moments; some people get them earlier and some others later, but we all have to experience them in order to understand the meaning of life. It also says that there is no reason to stress about what is going to happen because things happen for a reason and, even though you try to fight it, they will still happen.

I walk back to the guest house. As it is very dark outside, I decide to take the longest path to make sure I can walk through areas with light. When I get to the guest house I ask for Ramona's room so that I can check whether she wants to go for a drink. Quite funny, she is in room number three and I am in room number four. Coincidence? I don't think anything on this trip is a coincidence anymore.

Ramona's light is off, so I go to bed. I fall asleep really quickly.

Dear Blooming Me

Day 11: Wednesday - Ubud

I wake up and check the window to see if the weather is good. I have one day left in Bali and I want to get some sun to be tanned for the pink dress I will be wearing at my friend's wedding. I still cannot believe I am still white after two weeks here. Living in London has definitely changed my skin.

Good news! It has stopped raining and it seems there is some sun. I take a shower, get dressed and open the door of the room. To my surprise, Ramona is having breakfast at the table in front of her room, right next to mine.

I sit down next to her and ask the guest house service to bring my breakfast there. Ramona tells me that she is leaving Ubud this morning. She has been feeling sick and feels it is time to move to another city.

She tells me that she knows it's nothing serious because she has contacted her shaman, who connected with her energy and said that it would go away and she would feel better in the morning.

I cannot believe what I am hearing because it sounds crazy that someone can connect with your body when you call them by phone and tell you that you are going to be fine. But I do respect Ramona, so I listen to her and agree that if she does not feel she should stay in Ubud, then she should leave.

She has time before her taxi though, so I suggest she joins me in my first class of the day, 'Meditation for beginners'. She has no plans, so we finish breakfast and walk to Yoga Barn.

Talking to Ramona is incredibly relaxing. She makes me feel comfortable and safe. I feel I can say anything to her.

While we wait for the meditation class to start, Ramona tells me that she doesn't know if she wants to go back to her old job when she finishes her sabbatical. She is confused because, although she doesn't like to be in front of a computer all day, she does like the safety that she gets from it. She says that she doesn't want to give up on all the things she is learning from travelling. I can see her point, and I suggest she could find something in between: a different job doing something similar that gives her financial protection but complement it with going to yoga retreats or taking meditation classes.

This makes me think about 'me'. Do I like what I do? I don't know. I do like my corporate life. I like being ambitious and accomplishing challenges and I wouldn't like to change that. But, I have learnt how important it is to have a life balance and to be happy at work. The problem is that I am not sure if what I do fulfils me.

The class starts and the teacher explains to us how meditation works. This is very helpful because this is the first time I have been in a meditation class. She gives us two important instructions: first, it is ok to disconnect and have random thoughts; and second, it is ok if you cannot concentrate.

During meditation I try to concentrate and follow the voice of the teacher. However, my mind starts going away. I start thinking about how relaxing the room is. I look at the trees and the sun coming in and I think that I would like to get to know myself better. I want to learn how I am and how people perceive me. I think about asking ten friends from different environments to write down three to five characteristics that define me. Then, I could take those words and try to match them and, depending on the relationship I have with the person who wrote them, I could distinguish between what people think about me when they meet me and when they really know me.

I get so immersed in my own thoughts that, before I know it, the class is finished and I realise I have paid no attention to it.

***

We walk back to the guest house and I go to the swimming pool. It is time to start reading the Alchemist. I read this book a few years ago but I cannot remember the story. I order a tea, lie down on one of the sunbeds and open my book. I am very excited about reading it.

It is nearly eleven AM and Ramona comes to say goodbye. She gives me a piece of paper and asks me to give it to a guy called Paul who will walk past the swimming pool. We say goodbye and promise to keep in touch.

I start reading my book, highlighting some sentences that attract my attention. It's a great story and I would recommend anyone to read it. It is about a boy who one night, dreams about a treasure and decides to leave everything to find it. Depending on the moment in your life when you read the book, it will have a different meaning. In essence, it talks about signs, and the importance of following your instincts and never giving up. It couldn't be a better fit right now.

An hour later, a man walks past the swimming pool. He looks English, so I ask him if he is Paul. He gives me a weird look and I explain that Ramona asked me to give him her email address and her Facebook user name. He gives me the impression that he has a complex mind. He is probably very smart and doesn't trust people easily. He also pretends to be confident, but you can tell that he has insecurities. His hair is long on one side of the head and shorter on the other. He is intriguing.

He leaves but comes back ten minutes later.

He starts a conversation but, at the same time, he is checking his phone. I am not bothered about it, although he apologises a few times. He starts interrogating me and the conversation takes a strange turn. He judges me, calling me 'City girl', but I can sense that it is because the City thing attracts him. He also tells me that I have an 'Emma Stone' vibe when he has not even seen my eyes (I am wearing my sunglasses) and remarks that he loves her and her movie La La Land.

I ask him about himself. He works in computer security, from 2000-2003 in the City (in London), but he quit that life and has spent the last eight years living in South East Asia. He never went to University, taught himself how to hack computers and now works for corporations testing their security.

In his free time he does research into how energies interact in life. I am not sure I understand what he is talking about, but I am quite intrigued to learn about his research. I ask a few questions, but Paul does not give me much about his views or how everything works. He talks about the 'Seth Materials', and suggests I should read it. Then he changes topic, but again he does not give much away in any topic we start.

I take a listening approach. I feel that he wants to impress me somehow and I listen cautiously. He brags about how few hours he works per day and while my reaction would normally be to please, saying how jealous I am, this time I surprise myself by saying, "I am happy for you, but I don't get impressed by that. I like working."

> *I realise that by taking a listening approach, instead of leading the talk to make sure that I was making a good impression, I was learning more about him and also getting more time to process my thoughts and form my own view before giving an answer. And I liked it. It even made me feel more confident of what I was saying because instead of giving an answer with vague ideas I was giving my own views. It made me feel good and I was proud of it.*

My alarm rang, meaning it was time to get ready for my next yoga class. This is the Shamanic breathing class, pretty much the reason why I came back to Ubud. I say goodbye to Paul and walk once again to Yoga Barn.

The teacher giving the session is Leo, the same one who gave the excellent yoga class the week before. When I get to the class, he is organising some cards and putting incense around the room. He asks us to get comfortable and explains that this is a breathing exercise.

When we are all in the room, he says that we should look at this exercise as a journey, that each person will live a different trip, and not every time you do it will it be the same. He also says not to worry because every person joins the trip; some people at the beginning of the session, some closer to the end, but we all get there.

He says that if we are not ready for it, we should leave the room now. But if we decide to stay, we should not leave the room until the class is over. He mentions that we might cry or laugh and that we will hear the other people laughing or crying or making noises. I remind myself to get some tissues because I know I will definitely cry.

He asks us to get a card, but he does not give any further instructions. My card has the picture of a wolf. I leave it on the floor, next to my right leg. Leo explains that this is a breathing exercise and, therefore, the only thing we have to do is breathe: inhale and exhale at the speed of his clapping. While we breathe, he will put on some music. Some songs will have lyrics in English, some songs will just be made of sounds. He might also make some noise with a big drum.

Before we start, Leo suggests we get pillows or bed mats to be comfortable. I get a bed mat and grab some tissues from the bathroom. I am not expecting anything from this exercise because I don't think I can concentrate for a whole hour and a half. I lie down on the mat and try to relax and think about nothing.

I start breathing at the speed of Leo's claps: inhale, exhale, inhale, exhale and I focus on my breathing. Within what feels like seconds I feel some heat on my knees. I think it is energy, but I don't understand how I can have energy on my knees. It feels hot, but I don't know because I'm not touching my knees.

I have my eyes closed and I don't want to open them. I don't understand what is going on, but I can hear other people in the room making noises. I am curious about the other people, but I am more curious to understand what is going on with my body. Suddenly, I feel this energy expanding between my abdomen and my breast. I get worried as I don't want to damage my stomach, but I calm down thinking that I am just breathing – there is no harm in that.

I don't understand how this is happening, but I don't want it to stop. I wonder if I could stop it even if I wanted to. I keep focusing on my breathing and I start hearing my own mind saying words at the speed of my breathing. It says, 'Do not give up', 'Be strong', 'Be patient', 'Be happy', 'Run the extra mile', 'Fight for him', 'Be selfish'.

The heat goes to my head, but it doesn't stay there. It goes to my feet and legs. At the same time, I keep hearing the words.

Everything is becoming more intense. I am a bit scared, but I don't want it to stop. The heat goes to my arms and suddenly my hands feel locked and I can't move them. I can feel so much energy in my arms that I can feel them rising. I don't understand what is going on. I try to move my arms down but it's really hard. I don't open my eyes so I'm not sure that this is really happening. But, this is what I feel.

I keep hearing all the words in my head. Suddenly, when I hear 'Fight for him', a friend comes into my mind as a very clear image. This friend dated a guy who had commitment issues after his divorce. They broke up and, although he kept claiming that he didn't want to be with her, she was patient, had faith and never gave up on being together. A year later, they got back together and they are now extremely happy. But why am I thinking about her? Is this about Seb? Words keep coming into my mind. Now, when I hear 'Run the extra mile', I get my father's face.

Suddenly, Leo touches the upper part of my abdomen and says, "Relax." This is very intense. Then, he moves his hand to the back of my neck and says, "Calm down." I cannot move. He sits me up, moves me to the right a bit and moves his fingers up and down of my spine saying, "Let it go, it is ok." As soon as he says that, tears start dropping like a fountain.

Leo offers to bring me a tissue and the only thing I can say, without opening my eyes, is, "I cannot move my hands." I keep crying and feel all the energy leaving my body. I don't know how, but I feel relieved.

Words are still running through my head and, the moment I can move my hands a bit, I open my eyes, take The Alchemist and a pen from my bag, and write down all the words on the back of the book. I want to make sure I write them in the same order I heard them. I write:

'Don't give up'

'Be strong'

'Find yourself'

'Run the extra mile'

'Fight for him'

'Be selfish'

'Don't give up'

A few minutes later, Leo asks us to start coming back from the trip. I can barely listen to what he is saying. I am in shock. What did just happen? What are all these things about energy running through my body? I feel relaxed, but I am very confused.

The class forms into a circle to share thoughts, but no one mentions anything like what I have just lived. I cannot wait for the class to finish. I have many questions I want to ask Leo. What just happened cannot be real.

As soon as the class is over and Leo is alone, I approach him and ask, "What …?" but he finishes my sentence saying, "What did just happen?" "Yes! That was not normal." He looks at me and says, "It looked very normal to me. Your energy was connecting with your body." I tell him about the words and he asks if I wrote them down. When I say yes, he replies, "Good. Find the meaning of those words."

Knowing that he is not going to give me any more information than that, I leave the room and go to the cafeteria. There are some people from the class. I start talking to another woman who looks like she wants to share her experience. I cannot wait to hear it.

Unfortunately, her experience has nothing to do with mine. She felt like she had nails on her hands and head and went on a dream journey in which she was walking in a dessert with the animal that was on her card and she had to feed him so that he could keep her alive. Then, they finished up having a party on an island paradise.

I really don't understand anything. I don't believe in energies running through my body and even less in energy communicating with me. But what just happened was real. I have lived it. I am so confused that I cannot find an explanation.

I give up, accept that my brain is not capable of understanding it and decide to treat myself for the last time. I will get an hour's foot massage before my next class. I am still bewildered and in shock, but I decide to park my thoughts to one side and simply relax.

***

My next class is a sound meditation class. It seemed appealing when I first read about it, but I don't think anything can surpass the Shamanic breathing exercise. The teacher of the sound meditation class looks like Jesus Christ Superstar – black long hair, dressed in a long tunic. After a few minutes in the class I wonder, "What am I doing here?"

I am very sceptical but decide to give it a chance. He takes hours explaining everything and I barely listen to what he is saying. I look around. Everything looks very hippie. I check out the people, trying to find some similarities with me, but I can't see any. I have no idea what I'm doing there, but do try to engage.

The teacher starts singing and I follow him and the rest of the class. The song reminds me of when I was part of the church chorus at summer camp. I sing with the group and get deep into the song until I realise I am shouting to Seb in my mind saying, "Come back to me, I will take care of you and I will never leave you." What am I doing? What's wrong with me? The moment I realise what I am doing, I stop. From that point onwards, I cannot wait for the class to finish. I did not enjoy this experience.

***

I walk back to the guest house and when I get there, Kadek is already waiting for me to take me to Denpasar, the closest area to the airport. We buy some pizzas on the way; it is the least I can do for him after putting up with me the previous day.

During the trip, Kadek tells me more about his life. He rents the taxi, which costs him one million five hundred thousand rupiah per month (around eighty pounds). Some weeks he makes a profit, others he just makes enough to cover the rental. When he doesn't make money he tells his wife, "We have not been lucky this week."

When we get to the hotel, we give each other a hug and I give him a tip to get something nice for his wife. He is very happy and he says, "This money will bring food to the table." I wish I had more cash on me.

***

The hotel is disgusting. It is probably a hundred years old and dirty. The girl at reception tries to be pleasant but she is incredibly unhelpful. The bellboy walks me to the room, which is worse than the entrance.

I look at the sheets – old, dirty grey and home to two spiders. I am not sleeping here. I go back down to reception and ask for my money back and internet access. The girl at reception tries to tell me that I cannot use the hotel computer, but I don't give her any option. I take over the reception computer, book another hotel and ask for a taxi.

The new hotel is not miles better, but at least it is clean.

Dear Blooming Me

Day 12: Thursday – Despasar

Today is my last day in Bali. I really like this country, but I am ready to go home. I cannot wait to get to my hometown and see my parents and go to the wedding and see my friend walk down the aisle.

I pack everything into my bulky bag and take the van to the airport. The check-in queue is huge. Two hours later, I have to run to the plane because it is already past boarding time.

Once I am in my aisle seat, I check I have got everything with me and I start reading the Alchemist. I want to finish the book before I land in London to make it part of the Bali experience. I keep highlighting sentences:

> 'Never stop dreaming, follow your omens.'

> 'When you want something with all your heart, that's when you are closest to the Soul of the World. It is always a positive force.'

> 'We are afraid of losing what we have, whether it's our life or our possessions and property. But this fear evaporates when we understand that our life stories and the history of the world were written by the same hand.'

'The closer he got to the realisation of his dream, the more difficult things became. He was being constantly subjected to tests of his persistence and courage. If he pushed forward impulsively, he would fail to see the signs and omens left by God along his path.'

'Don't be impatient. Eat when it's time to eat. And move along when it's time to move along.'

'It was the language of enthusiasm, of things accomplished with love and purpose, and as part of a search for something believed in and desired.'

These are all very powerful sentences but, more importantly, they are meaningful to me. I just don't know what I have to do with them. I keep reading until suddenly one sentence makes me remember one of the phrases I wrote down at the Shamanic breathing exercise. 'Every search begins with beginner's luck. And every search ends with the victories being severely tested.' I write, 'Run the extra mile' next to it in the book.

What am I doing? I don't know. I wonder about the other sentences I had previously highlighted. I look back and I realise that I can link each of the sentences to the words I had written in the back of the book after the class: 'Don't give up', 'Be strong', 'Find yourself', 'Run the extra mile', 'Fight for him', 'Be selfish', 'Don't give up'.

I do this for a few pages and then I keep reading. This probably means something, but what? I don't understand. I keep reading but I cannot concentrate. My brain is speeding.

I have thousands of thoughts and I feel like everything starts to make sense. I need to write it down:

Four years ago, Mum was deeply sad and depressed before she had her second stroke. If she had not had it, maybe she would still be sad. Her stroke gave her a second chance to enjoy life. Since her stroke, she doesn't worry about silly things and forgets quickly the things that upset her. She is happy again and it has made my parents fall in love one more time.

However, Mum's stroke tested the roots of our family and we failed. At the time, we were not capable of understanding each other or being there for each other and, as a consequence, we fell apart.

Pilar Sordo says in her book Bienvenido Dolor that cancer cures. When I read that I smiled. I think that, a year later, my cancer came to cure us. You might think I have now lost it completely, but, I honestly think it brought closeness between my brother and me. I think that when we learnt about my cancer, Tony got scared of losing me and, although he still had not overcome his issues with me over Mum's sickness, he did not want to waste more time being mad at me. My cancer also helped Mum to step up again in her recovery; she took back her role as a mother. And I think it also helped Dad and Tony to start talking again.

If I had not had cancer, I would probably not have realised how lucky I am. I would probably not have realised how much my family and my friends love me or how unconditional is their support for me.

Mum, Dad and Tony are the most important people in my life and probably the ones to whom I tell the least. I need to tell them more often how much I love them. It is so silly how the people we love the most are the ones we tell the least.

My cancer also made me quit smoking and drinking. If I had continued smoking, I would never have met Seb (Seb would never date a, what he calls, 'stinky person'). Being with Seb helped me to overcome my commitment issues and understand what I want: to share my life with a special someone who wants to be my partner, build a future together, and who will love me so much that he would find the only reason to love me when all the odds are against it.

The breakup made me sad. Normally I would pretend to be strong and deal with it without exteriorising it. However, I was scared that I could damage my stomach. So, for the first time in my life, I let myself be sad and I contacted a psychologist a few days after the split to help me look at things with perspective. And she did.

In the first session I realised that my sadness had nothing to do with my breakup, but was the result of the huge baggage of problems and fears I have been carrying for years. The psychologist has helped me organise my thoughts, understand my problems and learn how to look at life from another perspective. The process has shown me how important is to put myself first and think about how I feel about things.

By listening to myself I realised that I needed time on my own to disconnect from everything. I needed to clear my thoughts and put things into perspective. That is why I booked my trip to Bali.

Bali helped me learn about myself, who I am, what I want. But most importantly, it has helped me learn about my biggest weakness: my tendency to devalue myself. I have realised that I never recognise the things I do well and I give myself a hard time over things I don't excel in. I focus on the 'Bs', just like my father did when I would get home with my grades from school.

***

I smile. Everything makes sense now. I don't know how, but I now see it very clearly. This is insane, but I guess that everything happens for a reason.

All of the sudden, I am full of energy. There are many things I want to do and achieve. I write them down so that I don't forget.

I feel so lucky to have had the opportunity to experience this. It is funny to think that if any person had asked me during the trip what I thought about this experience, I would have said, "It is ok but travelling alone is not my thing." However, now, although I would still agree that travelling alone is not my thing, I feel like this has been the best experience of my life.

With a smile on my face I keep reading the Alchemist. All the sentences I read just reassure me about what I have just realised. I am convinced I need to follow my instincts, fight for what I want and never give up. There is a destiny written for me but things take time to happen. And in the meantime, I need to follow the words from the Shamanic breathing exercise. First, I need to be strong and don't give up. Then, I need to focus on finding myself.

***

A few hours later, I land in Doha. I still have a great big smile on my face and I feel I have made a major discovery in my life. I feel strong, motivated and happy. But most importantly, I want to believe in faith. Having faith makes me happy.

I have a couple of hours between flights, so I log onto one of the computers. I open Facebook and the first thing I see is a picture of Seb with some of his friends. Really? Of all the posts I can get on my Facebook feed, does Seb have to be the first one? Seeing him in that picture smiling and having a beer at a pub in London makes me sad. This is the last thing I want to see at this moment.

I log off and walk around the airport. I am so upset. I don't want to see or hear anything about Seb.

All my previous enthusiasm and strength disappear. I am so angry at myself. What was I thinking? Faith? Destiny? Signs? How can I actually believe in these things? I work in Finance. I believe in numbers and facts. Bali has been a great experience, but it is not real life. In real life there are problems, disappointments and hard moments. I know it feels great to believe in destiny and faith, but there is nothing that proves that they are real.

I walk up and down the airport for half an hour. I keep blaming myself for being such an idiot and letting myself believe in all these things. When, suddenly, I think about the wolf. What does the wolf on the Shamanic breathing card mean? I find a computer and Google: "Wolf Shamanic Breathing." It says:

1. Sharp intelligence, deep connection with instincts

2. Appetite for freedom

3. Expression of strong instincts

4. Feeling threatened, lack of trust in someone or in yourself

I smile. It is my choice. And I choose to have faith.

Conclusion

During the last couple of months, I have been sharing this story with close friends and family. Partly because I feel very proud of what I have learnt, but also because every time I have told the story I have learnt something new. Either something new would make sense, or someone would tell me about their experience or recommend a book that would be helpful. You would be surprised how many people have also had a cathartic moment and have kept it to themselves for fear of being called crazy.

It has been quite interesting to see how people react when I tell them the story. Some nodded while I was talking because they have lived something similar. Some others would not believe what I was saying but would respect it because they know me and they know that I would not make it up. Only a few would change the topic because they don't believe in these things.

My favourite reaction came from my father. It was two days after I had landed from Bali and I was at my parents' house in the north of Spain. I woke up at eight AM and, as usual, I went straight to my parents' room to wake them up. I gave them a good morning kiss and Dad said, "You have not told me anything about Bali yet." I told him it was a long story and he said he had time. So I sat down on his bed, and spent the next hour and a half telling him all about my trip. He listened to it quietly.

I was a bit nervous – especially when I told him about the Shamanic breathing experience – I thought he was going to think I had gone crazy (I would probably think that myself, had I not experienced it). However, he said nothing. The only comment he made was after I told him about my conversation with Paul at the swimming pool. He said, "I repeat what I have always told you, be yourself."

Later that day, Dad approached me while I was sunbathing on the terrace and said, "It is a fantastic story you told me this morning." He did not say anything else, but hearing that made me feel good.

When I left for Bali, my intention was to forget about my ex-boyfriend. However, the trip has done so much more. It has helped me deal with issues and fears I had been dragging around for the last few years, some of which I didn't even know existed. The trip has made me remember that things happen for a reason; the only thing is, we often learn about that reason in the future.

Since I came back, I have been trying to understand the reason why I had this life affirming experience. First, I thought it was because it was about time I processed all the things that have happened to me in the last five years. People deal with their issues at different times, so maybe I required five years to deal with my mum's stroke and my cancer.

Then, I thought that it happened because I had to find myself. It was the third task on the words I wrote down at the Shamanic breathing exercise, so maybe it was a sign. So, I focused all my time and energy on reading books, such as The Power of Now[6] and Reinventarse[7] (Reinventing Yourself), and on listening and analysing myself. I even had a biological decoding session by Skype with a professional in Argentina. Biological decoding is a way of decoding any type of symptom (physical, emotional or mental) and resolving them by identifying the emotional shock that caused it. It sounds daft, I know, but it helped.

All the books I have read have helped me to understand that life is all about attitude. We have a destiny, but we are the only ones who can control what makes us happy.

I have also realised how important it is to live the moment (the now) instead of living in the past or the future. Living in the past makes us feel sad as we regret what we did, what we could have done. While living in the future makes us stressed or anxious as we expect things that we cannot control. This last one is me – I have a tendency to live in the future, stressing about the things I want, and worrying about not knowing if they are going to happen. But most importantly, these books and the people I have met on the way have helped me remember to never give up on my dreams. If I really want something, it will happen. I cannot explain how it works, but it simply does. And if you don't believe me – just try it. Just make sure your fears don't take over.

---

[6] Eckhart Tolle, The Power of Now (Yellow Kite, 2016).
[7] Dr. Mario Alonso Puig, Reinventarse. Tu segunda oportunidad (Plataforma Editorial, 2010).

Although working through my burdens and finding myself were part of the process, I now know the real reason why I had my cathartic moment. I needed to sort all my previous issues in order to be strong to deal with the hardest moment of my life: my father's death. On the 18th August 2017 my father passed away. It was an unexpected death. He woke up with my mum that morning, and two hours later, he had a heart attack. He was only sixty-seven years old.

I think I needed to understand what my father had told me three years earlier when one of his best friends passed away: "Life is hard, but we need to keep going." Unfortunately, we all go through difficult moments in life, some experiencing them earlier, some later. But we all go through them to make us strong and understand the meaning of life.

I honestly do not think I would have been able to cope if my father had left three months ago, before my trip to Bali. There is a high chance that I would have become depressed, thinking that everything happens to me and wondering what I have done wrong to deserve it.

Now, I look at it in a way my father would be proud. Although his death leaves a huge hole in me, and I am extremely sad because I am realising what it means to never be able to hug him again, I look at it with happiness.

I am happy because he had a great life and enjoyed every minute of it. I am happy because he did not suffer and his last days were good days. I am happy because I am proud of being his daughter and I have been lucky to learn from him. I am happy because I have so many good memories of him. But it hurts to know I will not be able to create new ones. It hurts to know that no-one will ever love me as much as he did, or that I will not be able to see how his face lights up every time he sees me walking through the airport exit. However, I am accepting that I need to honour his name and keep making him proud. I have made my goal to enjoy life and to make the best of each day.

Dear Blooming Me

THANK YOU

I am honored that you have chosen Dear Blooming Me and I sincerely hope that you enjoyed it.

If you would like to stay in touch, I invite you to visit my webpage www.amadorafernandez.com.

www.ingramcontent.com/pod-product-compliance
Lightning Source LLC
Chambersburg PA
CBHW022107040426
42451CB00007B/155